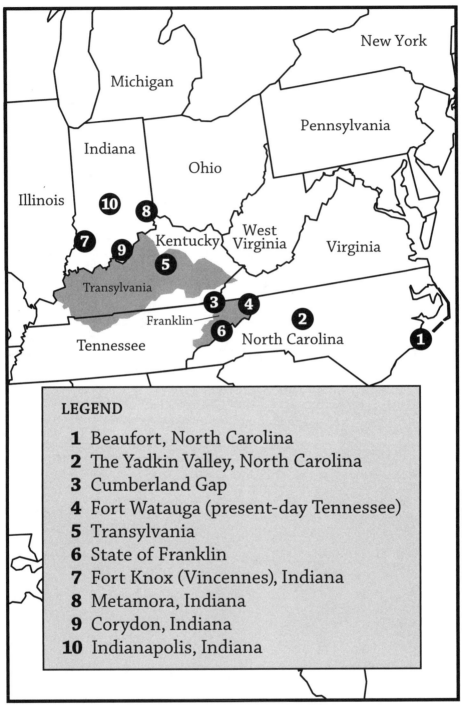

LEGEND

1 Beaufort, North Carolina
2 The Yadkin Valley, North Carolina
3 Cumberland Gap
4 Fort Watauga (present-day Tennessee)
5 Transylvania
6 State of Franklin
7 Fort Knox (Vincennes), Indiana
8 Metamora, Indiana
9 Corydon, Indiana
10 Indianapolis, Indiana

Locations featured in Cody Carter's journey

THE CARTER JOURNALS

TIME TRAVELS IN EARLY U.S. HISTORY

SHANE PHIPPS

Indiana Historical Society Press | Indianapolis 2015

Printed in the United States of America

This book is a publication of the
Indiana Historical Society Press
Eugene and Marilyn Glick Indiana History Center
450 West Ohio Street
Indianapolis, Indiana 46202-3269 USA
www.indianahistory.org
Telephone orders 1-800-447-1830
Fax orders 1-317-234-0562
Online orders @ http://shop.indianahistory.org

The paper in this publication meets the minimum requirements of American National Standard for Information Sciences—Permanence of Paper for Printed Library Materials, ANSI Z39. 48–1984 ⊛

Library of Congress Cataloging-in-Publication Data
Phipps, Shane.
The Carter journals : time travels in early U.S. history / Shane Phipps.
      pages cm
Audience: Grades 7 to 8.
Includes bibliographical references and index.
ISBN 978-0-87195-365-0 (cloth : alkaline paper) — ISBN 978-0-87195-364-3 (paperback : alkaline paper)
1. North Carolina—Description and travel—Juvenile literature. 2. Franklin (State)—Description and travel—Juvenile literature. 3. Indiana—Description and travel—Juvenile literature. 4. Carter family—Diaries—Juvenile literature. 5. Carter family—Travel—North Carolina—Juvenile literature. 6. Carter family—Travel—Indiana—Juvenile literature. 7. North Carolina—History—Colonial period, ca. 1600–1775—Juvenile literature. 8. Indiana—History—19th century—Juvenile literature. I. Title.

F257.P44 2015
917.5604—dc23
                              2015007132

The Carter Journals is made possible
through the generous support of
Wanda Y. Fortune.

Contents

Preface

I teach United States history to eighth graders. Some days I do a better job than others. Over my years in the classroom, I have discovered that my students usually learn best when I can come up with stories to tell them that go along with, or add to, the material in their textbook. For this reason, I am continually looking to further educate myself about the material I cover, which happens to be colonial America through the Civil War.

I look for stories that enhance what is in the textbook. I love it when I can find some little tidbits of information on the periphery of mainstream history, much like the famous broadcaster Paul Harvey's essays called "The Rest of the Story." When I can take my students off the beaten path of mainstream history with stories that don't get as much coverage, their understanding and appreciation of the textbook is deepened.

When I started teaching, I realized that most of my students didn't have a great deal of affection for history. They found it boring and pointless. Granted, if history is taught straight from textbooks as endless dates and battles, it can get a little dry for some folks' tastes, even mine. The key is finding ways to make history come alive and, if at all possible, to make it connect to your life. Whether we are conscious of it or not, we are all connected through history. Our ancestors wrote our history—they lived it. Too often, we are all guilty of losing sight of that.

A couple of years ago, I began to long for a book that my students might like to read—a book that paralleled the time line of what I teach, but which told stories in a more entertaining way than most history textbooks. I wanted to find a book that I could use in my classroom to lead my students off the well-worn trails of the textbook material to where we could stop and smell the roses around the edges of the stories—to learn and be entertained. I then had a very interesting notion: Instead of looking for such a book, why not just write it myself? I had always played with the idea of being a writer, but had never really pursued it. So I did it.

This is a work of historical fiction. Historical fiction is my favorite genre. I have learned a great deal of what I know about history from these types of books. Readers should know going into a book like this that it is not meant to be 100 percent accurate in every aspect. This book blends real people and events with fictional characters, events, and dialogue. While much research was done in setting as accurate a historical background for my story as possible, this is still my version of the events.

Readers should recognize many of the "mainstream" stories in this book. I use them to provide the proper context for other events that are not so well known, but that are to me no less important parts of America's story. There is only so much room in our history textbooks, and therefore, publishers can't possibly squeeze every story worth telling into them. I wanted to bring out some of the stories that don't get told and place them in their rightful spot in the big picture.

While this book is primarily aimed at a teenage audience, I hope that adults will find it entertaining and informative as well. This is the type of book that can be read a little at a time or in one sitting. If you are looking for an epic that goes into minute details and exhausts a single subject, then you have come to the wrong place. I wrote this book specifically for those with short attention spans in mind. If you prefer a book that bounces along from scene to scene and era to era, digging up little nuggets of forgotten history along the way, then read on.

So the real purpose of this book—my not-so-hidden agenda—is to spark an interest in someone who doesn't think he or she has an interest in history. Enjoy traveling through history with Cody Carter. When you learn of some event that you weren't aware of, do yourself a favor and dig a little deeper on your own. You may just be surprised at how much you really do like history.

Acknowledgments

First and foremost, I want to thank God for the many blessings He has given me. Without His guiding hand, I never would have had the ability to complete this project. (Philippians 4:13)

A big thanks to Jan Dorsey. Jan is a language arts teacher at my school. I wanted to have an "editor on the fly" to help me catch any mistakes and to make suggestions on how to make improvements to the book. I knew I could count on Jan to give me honest and critical feedback. Every time I would hammer out another chapter, I would run it down to Jan, and she would generally have it edited for me in a day or two. I really appreciate her efforts.

I would also like to thank my sister-in-law, Jeanne Stafford-Phipps, and my niece, Meredith Phipps. I would e-mail them new chapters and they would give me feedback. Meredith was in fourth grade at the time, so I used her as a gauge to make sure younger readers would be able to understand and appreciate the story.

Bruce Simon was my mentor teacher when I first started teaching history. He instilled in me the importance of reading as much as I could about the subject I teach. He also left me with many of his books when he retired. Thank you, Bruce.

I want to thank my parents, Hugh and Becky Phipps, for being so supportive and encouraging during the process of writing the book. They too read the chapters as I finished them, and their suggestions and feedback were valuable.

Special thanks to my wife, Jeanna, and my daughter, Molly. They were very supportive of me at home and put up with me as I would often sit and write the story "in my head" while not being particularly attentive to them sometimes. I love you both.

I would also like to thank several people at the Indiana Historical Society Press for their work. Thanks to Ray Boomhower. When I first had the concept of the book, I e-mailed Ray, whom I remembered from when I worked part time at the IHS History Market years ago while in college. Ray saw potential in my idea and put me in touch with the proper people. Thanks to Elaine Rosa for helping me through the writing of the curriculum guide that goes with the book. Special thanks to Teresa Baer for believing in the project, all her work in the editing process, and mostly just for putting up with and supporting the needs of a first-time author. Thanks as well to the IHS Press staff who checked the facts, gathered the illustrations, and edited the book: Rachel Popma, Chelsea Sutton, Karen Wood, and Jennifer Banning.

Last but not least, I want to dedicate this book to my grandfather, Harry Phipps. He was the basis for Cody's Grandpa Carter. He and my maternal grandfather, Olen McGinnis, who passed away years ago, were largely responsible for my love of history. Thankfully, Grandpa got to read my final draft of The Carter Journals. Sadly, he passed away on October 6, 2011 (aged ninety), before the book went to print, but he knew that it was going to be published and he was very proud of that. I am very proud of him.

Introduction

Cody Carter sat in the living room of his suburban Indianapolis home spellbound at the stories the old man was telling. The man was Cody's paternal grandfather, John Carter, visiting Indiana from his home in Hawkins County, Tennessee. Cody loved to hear his grandfather tell tales because they usually were about his own family. The stories also usually revolved around history, which just happened to be Cody's favorite subject in school. "Grandpa Carter is like a walking history book," Cody would brag to his friends, who usually seemed unimpressed. Cody, now fourteen and in the eighth grade, often wondered why he seemed to be in the minority when it came to his love of history. Most of his friends just complained about history class. They said it was boring and pointless. *Maybe*, Cody thought, *it's because they don't have a Grandpa Carter.*

Grandpa Carter had always impressed upon Cody the importance of understanding your place in history. Thanks to his grandfather's stories, Cody had a better appreciation for history. Sometimes it seemed like history was something that only happened in faraway places to long-ago people. Sometimes history didn't seem very relevant. But when Cody heard Grandpa's stories, he felt like he was being drawn into the historical time line. He could relate history to his own family.

Grandpa Carter once told Cody that the Carter family had come to America from England back in the colonial times. The name Carter meant "driver of carts," so apparently, the English Carters must have been in that business way back when. Grandpa Carter had a wealth of material from which to draw his tales. The Carter family, it seemed, had always had a passion for recording their lives in the form of journals. It had become a time-honored family tradition for the Carters to keep journals, usually beginning when they were teenagers, and to pass them down to the next generation. When the Carter teens came of age, they also received the journals of the young Carters that had come before them. So as they started to record their own histories, they could also begin reading the histories of their teenage ancestors. This had kept more than a few Carter children very interested in history classes through the years. History means a lot more when you can trace your place in it.

Just now, Cody was learning about the day when his grandpa had begun his own journal. The year was 1944. John Carter was a thirteen-year-old who was forced into the role of the man of the house. His dad, Will Carter, had been called to service in the U.S. Army. John was forced to temporarily drop out of the eighth grade so he could help his mother and younger sister run the family's small tobacco and cattle farm just outside of Rogersville, Tennessee. It was the very same one-hundred-acre mountain farm that Cody now loved to go and visit, but it was a tough life for a teenaged boy in 1944.

Cody sat and listened to Grandpa's story, but he had heard some of this before. The stories that Cody really wanted to dig into were those in the box of old journals that Grandpa had brought to Indiana to leave in Cody's possession. The journals had come down through the family from the very first generation of Carters in America—all the way back to 1730. Tomorrow, Cody planned to go right for the oldest one and begin working his way straight through the whole box.

PART ONE

The Journal of Edward Carter
Beaufort, North Carolina, 1730

1

Cody woke up early the next morning. It was a Saturday, and he wasn't used to waking up before ten o'clock on the weekends. But he'd been too excited to sleep. All night he had dreamed about what he might discover in that box of dusty old journals. Cody ran downstairs to see if Grandpa had left yet and was happy to see he was still sitting down eating breakfast. "Well, Cody, I didn't expect you'd see me off this mornin'," Grandpa said.

"I guess I was too excited to sleep in very late," Cody replied. "I'm not sure my brain ever did go to sleep. I just hope those journals are half as exciting as my dreams—I had some real whoppers!"

Grandpa Carter leaned back and wiped a little bit of pancake syrup from the corner of his mouth with a napkin. "I reckon I don't know what you dreamed about, but those journals are about real life. Real life ain't always excitin', but I guarantee it's always educational, at least if you're payin' attention," he said in his southern mountain drawl. "I expect there will be enough excitement in them to keep you well occupied, though." The old man rose from the table. "Well, I have a six-and-a-half-hour drive ahead of me. Better get a move on—these old bones don't like long car rides like they once did."

"Summer vacation is right around the corner, Grandpa," said Cody as he followed his grandfather to the door. "We'll be down to visit real soon."

"I'll be lookin' forward to it, Cody," replied Grandpa. "Oh, and one more thing: Don't let those journals pull you away from your school work now, you hear?"

"I won't," replied Cody, almost believing himself.

Grandpa got into his car, waved, and drove off. Cody normally felt sad when his grandfather left, but right now he was too eager to go through the journals to be sad.

Cody ran upstairs to his bedroom, where he had left the box of journals. He dug down to the bottom to retrieve the oldest one. It was leather bound, about the size of a paperback book. The leather was dry and crackled. Cody noticed that the book had a very old smell. A strong feeling suddenly came over him. *These books are important and they are fragile*, he thought. *I had better treat these like I am borrowing them from a museum.* He carefully opened the front cover and looked at the title page. The pages themselves were in surprisingly good shape—a little bit yellow, but they seemed pretty sturdy. Cody was a little relieved that the book wasn't so brittle that it would shatter into dust the moment he turned the page. He suspected that other family members before him had felt the same feelings of responsibility that had just come over him. "This book has been well taken care of," Cody heard himself whisper.

Cody read the words on the title page: *The Journal of Edward Carter . . . Beaufort, North Carolina . . . 1730.* "Wow!" He paused to do a little mental math. "This thing is over 280 years old!" he exclaimed.

With great anticipation, Cody turned the page. He realized he was about to be transported almost three centuries back in time. He was about to relive the lives of some of his relatives when they were about his age.

What Cody didn't realize was just how true this was. Cody Carter was about to take a very strange trip.

Cody began to read the words at the top of the journal's first page.

I am Edward Carter. I am fourteen years of age. I live in Beaufort, North Carolina, with my mother and father, Elizabeth and Edward Sr. . . .

Cody started to feel strange. As he continued to read, he felt as if he were falling down a deep, spinning mine shaft, or on a roller coaster, twisting through a dark tunnel. Suddenly, he stopped cold. Shaking the cobwebs out of his head, he looked around and found himself in a very small room in a very small house. He had what appeared to be a feather in his hand, but the pointed end of the feather was dripping with black ink. Cody recognized it as a quill pen used for writing back in olden times. He was sitting on a wooden stool in front of a desk with a tilted top. He seemed to have just finished writing in a black, leather-bound journal. The journal looked very much like the very book he had just been reading, only much, much newer. The room was fairly dark except for some light pouring through a window a few feet away. The floors of the house were wooden, and the room was sparsely furnished. What furniture there was appeared to be handmade of wood. A large stone fireplace along one wall seemed to be open to another room on the other side.

Cody looked down and saw that he was wearing different clothes. They were not his own, that was for sure. He had on black leather shoes and long white socks that stretched clear up past his knees and were tucked up under his brown pants, which Cody immediately recognized as knickers. His shirt was white and had very puffy sleeves. He was also wearing a vest. It was certainly not an outfit Cody would have picked out for himself, unless maybe it was for Halloween.

Cody heard some metallic sounds coming from the room on the other side of the fireplace. He sheepishly tiptoed toward the doorway between the two rooms and slowly peeked around the edge of the door opening. He saw a woman cooking over a black iron woodstove. She jumped back, obviously startled at the head peeking around at her. "Oh my, Edward dear! You near scared the life out of your poor old mother!" the woman exclaimed, in a sort of accent that seemed a cross between British and southern. "What are you doing, sneaking around like that, lad?" she said.

Edward? Who was Edward? "I'm not Edward, ma'am. My name is Cody," Cody replied.

"Cody is it, you say now?" the woman answered. "Well, your father Edward Sr. will be most disappointed to hear that. I suggest you come to your senses and tend to your chores before he gets back from the fields, *Edward!*" she said impatiently.

Cody was completely confused now. Had he even awakened this morning at all? Was this just another of his dreams? He decided not to push it any further and to play along until he woke up for real. "Yes, ma'am. What chores need to be done, exactly?" Cody inquired.

"The wood needs splittin', of course. Don't you remember your pa telling you before he left?" she replied.

"Oh, yeah. I guess I was too wrapped up in my journal and sort of lost track of time. I will get right to it," Cody answered.

"See that you do. If your pa comes back and sees that pile of unsplit wood out there, it will be your hide he'll be tannin'," she said.

Cody—or was it Edward?—headed outside and found a large pile of logs with an axe leaning against it. His chore was clear, and it wasn't the kind of work he was used to, although he had helped his grandpa split some wood in Tennessee before, just enough to know it was not going to be easy.

He took a good long look at his surroundings. Cody realized he had actually been here before. He and his family had vacationed in the Outer Banks of North Carolina a couple of times, and he had visited the historic little village of Beaufort. Much of it here looked the same, except it was not nearly as big and spread out. As he looked around, he realized that, at this point, it wasn't "Historic Beaufort." It was just Beaufort.

The Carters' little house sat away from town, but Cody could look out over the town and see the little port where the fishing boats docked. He remembered taking a boat tour in Beaufort and seeing dolphins swimming around right near the town. He wondered if there were dolphins down there now. Looking across the channel, he saw an island. Cody remembered that there were wild horses on that island that were descendants of the ones who had come to America with the Spanish explorers. He felt an odd comfort that they must be there now too, at least something a little familiar in this strange situation.

As he gazed at the little town in the distance, trying to get his bearings and make sense out of all this, Cody remembered his chore and set out to get it done. He picked up one of the logs and set it on its end on a level spot of ground. He grabbed the axe and took aim at the center of the log cut. THWACK. The axe found its mark, and the log cracked open and fell into two halves. Cody felt a sense of pride at his accomplishment. "That wasn't so tough," he boasted. Then he looked at the large pile of logs that remained to be split. "I have a feeling that by the time I get to the bottom of that pile, I won't be so cocky," he said to himself. With determination and a little dread, he reached for another log and continued his task.

The afternoon light was beginning to fade when Cody picked up the last log. He calculated that he had been at it for at least two hours. His hands were sore and red, and little blisters were beginning to form on them. He heard a man's voice calling. "Edward, how is the splittin' comin' along? I allowed you'd be done before now."

Cody looked up and saw a large man walking toward him, evidently from a long day of working in the fields. *That must be Edward's dad*, he thought. "I got a bit of a late start, but I am just about finished now," he said.

Edward Carter Sr. looked down at the boy with a bit of a devilish smile. "And what, might I ask, delayed you?" he asked.

Cody was a little nervous. He wondered just what kind of a father he was dealing with here. Was he in trouble? Had Elizabeth Carter been joking or serious when she made that hide tanning remark? He decided he had better play it straight and take his chances. "I was writing in my journal, sir. I lost track of the time."

"Well, now, a journal is a fine thing, and I am right proud of you for takin' it on, but an oil lamp is a fine thing for writin' once the sun goes down, that is.

The good Lord provides us daylight for splittin' wood," Edward Sr. replied.

Cody was relieved that he didn't seem to be in for a "hide tannin'." Edward Sr. seemed to be a fair kind of father, much like his own usually was. "Yes, sir," Cody replied. "I will keep that in mind."

"Very well, then. Let's get washed up for supper, and after we eat, I will tell you a tale that you will surely want to put in your journal. It's about the time when you were two years old and met the famous pirate Blackbeard, right here in Beaufort," Edward Sr. said.

Well, this should be interesting, thought Cody, as he followed Edward Sr. into the house for supper.

As he sat down at the little table in the kitchen, Cody's head was swimming with questions that he could not ask. He realized that he had to play the part of Edward Carter Jr., but he wondered how long this was going to last. When would he wake up, or be transported back to his bedroom . . . or would he? There were just too many possibilities for him to even consider. This seemed way too real to be a dream. In a way, Cody hoped that it was not a dream because it was certainly a fantastic trip. He only feared the uncertainty of it all. He longed to know how this would all play out.

The table was set with a lovely spread of food. There were green beans, potatoes, corn bread, and some sort of meat that looked like roast beef. "We are nearly out of venison," Elizabeth said, looking at Edward Sr.

"Well, now, Junior and I will have to see to that little problem tomorrow, won't we, son?" he replied.

Cody knew that venison was deer meat. He had actually gone deer hunting with his dad in Indiana, but he had never succeeded in killing one yet. The idea of going deer hunting with Edward Sr. excited him.

"Yes, sir, Pa," Cody replied. It felt more than a little strange saying that. First of all, he had never called anyone Pa before, and second, this wasn't really his father. But Cody was starting to get into this role.

The food was very good, and Cody stuffed himself, having worked up quite a big appetite from all that wood splitting. He was looking forward to hearing the Blackbeard story. He remembered seeing something about Blackbeard in a maritime museum when he had been in Beaufort. Could it really be that one of his relatives actually met this infamous pirate?

After the supper dishes were washed and put away, Cody and Edward Sr. went into the main room of the little house. Edward Sr. sat in a wooden rocking chair and lit his pipe. Cody sat on the stool in front of the slant-topped desk. He was not sure how eager to appear. He decided to let Edward Sr. start the conversation, even though he was dying to ask about Blackbeard.

The room filled with the rather strong aroma of pipe smoke. Cody wanted to say something about the dangers of smoking, but stopped himself. *This guy has been dead for more than two hundred years. A little pipe smoke won't hurt him*, he thought to himself, a wry little smile crossing his lips at this amusing notion. A moment later, Edward Sr. finally began to speak. "Well, I guess you are waitin' for a story, eh?" he said.

"Yes, sir. Did I really meet Blackbeard?" Cody replied.

"As sure as I live and breathe my boy, though you were a might too young to remember," said Edward Sr. "The year was 1718. You would have been just about two years old. Blackbeard had been in command of his ship *Queen Anne's Revenge* for about a year or so. Oh, he was a rascal, he was. His ship had forty guns mounted to her, and he had a crew, they say, of about three hundred men. They were sailing up and down the coast of North and South Carolina just pillagin' and plunderin' up a storm. Why, just the week before he came to Beaufort, he and his crew blockaded the port of Charles Towne. They held that whole town for ransom and got away with a sight of booty, too!"

Cody sat in rapt attention as Edward Sr. continued.

"Once they left Charles Towne, they sailed north and into Topsail Inlet, right here in Beaufort. They ran the *Queen Anne's Revenge* aground on one of those little sandbar islands out there. Blackbeard left most of his men marooned out there and with a few others came into Beaufort on a small boat. They were needin' some supplies and came lookin' for the mercantile. Well, that is right where I happened to be, and I just happened to be totin' you at my side. I was twenty years old then and was just gettin' our little farm off the ground. I was tryin' to establish a line of credit at the mercantile, and you were tryin' to talk me into buyin' you a stick of hard candy, as usual. I heard a commotion outside the door, and then I saw him, the famous Edward Teach, better known as Blackbeard, the pirate."

Cody was literally on the edge of his seat, so much so that had to catch himself from tipping forward and falling over. "What did he look like?" he asked.

"Let me tell you, he was the kind of feller that you don't forget. He was fearsome lookin'. He was tall, but he gave you the impression that he was even taller. His clothes were eye catchin'. He wore black leather boots all the way up to his knees. He had dark clothes except for a bright crimson coat. At his sides were two menacin' looking swords, and across his chest stretched bandoleers stuffed plumb full with pistols and knives. On his head sat a wide-brimmed black hat, and under that hat was long jet-black hair. Legend has it that he used to tuck cannon fuses under that hat and light them just before doin' battle so that he would look even more frightful. But his most strikin' feature was on his face—his black beard. It was somethin' to behold! It was long and black and he had it braided into several pigtails with little shiny red ribbons tied in them. Blackbeard didn't have to say a word to get noticed. Just the sight of him walkin' into a room would make folks stand at attention and make the hair stand up on the backs of their necks."

As Edward Sr. finished his vivid description of Blackbeard, Cody thought he felt the hair bristle up on the back of his own neck. The idea of pirates had always seemed like it was from some fictional book or movie, but here he was sitting across the room from a man who was eyewitness to the most notorious pirate of them all. "So what did Blackbeard do when he walked into the store?" Cody asked.

"Well, there is where the story sort of loses a bit of drama," replied Edward Sr. "He walked up to the counter and explained to the storekeeper that he needed some provisions for his crew. He listed off what he needed and waited there while his order was filled. While he was standin' there, he introduced himself to me as Edward Teach, and I told him our names and we shook hands. He reached down and tousled your hair and remarked about what a fine, strappin' lad you were. So there we all were just standin' around, three Edwards, one of us a notorious pirate, one of us a frightened and awestruck young farmer, and one of us was you."

Edward Sr. paused for a long moment to relight his pipe. "What happened then?" Cody asked impatiently.

"Not much, really," replied Edward Sr. "The shop-keep brought all the goods to the front of the store, and Blackbeard paid him in gold coins, bowed and tipped his hat, and walked back out the door. If a feller didn't know any better, they would have thought he was a gentleman."

"You mean he didn't steal anything?" Cody asked.

"Nope. I reckon he saved all his plunderin' for the high seas!" replied Edward Sr. with a chuckle. "It was just later that same year that ol' Blackbeard reached his end. He had sailed on up the coast here aways and made his home

A woodcut of Captain Teach, alias Blackbeard. Blackbeard is shown wearing clothing similar to that described by Edward Carter Jr.'s father.

base on Ocracoke Island. Well, he was hunted down by a British vessel commanded by a man by the name of Maynard. Maynard planned a little surprise for ol' Mr. Blackbeard, and he and his men overtook their vessel. Maynard shot Blackbeard in the skirmish and wounded him badly. Some of Maynard's men finished him off. They cut ol' Blackbeard's head off and ran it up one of the sail masts for the whole world to look at. They threw the rest of him overboard, and they claim his headless body swam around the boat for a while before sinkin' to the bottom." Edward Sr. sat back, apparently finished with his tale.

Cody could hardly believe what he had heard. Even though it had been an exhilarating tale, he felt himself beginning to get a bit sleepy. It had been a pretty eventful day, to say the least. He turned and glanced at the journal that still lay open on the desk. He reached for it and closed the cover. As he did so, a curtain seemed to open before his eyes. He felt that same strange swimming sensation in his head and butterflies in his stomach. After a moment in which he seemed to black out, Cody opened his eyes and found himself back in his own bedroom in Indianapolis. He glanced back at the journal and saw that it was opened to a page where young Edward Carter had written of meeting Blackbeard when he was two years old.

2

Cody did not know what to make of the situation. What had just happened? He had pretty much ruled out a dream. Was it a hallucination? Perhaps it was something he ate, or maybe he was coming down with something. Cody was sure there must be some reasonable explanation. He could not possibly have just gone through what it seemed he had gone through. He decided it would be best if he took a little break from journal reading.

Later that evening, after a mediocre supper of leftover spaghetti, Cody excused himself to his bedroom. He was surprised to find himself dealing with a case of nerves. *Why am I so nervous?* he thought. *I am only going to read an old journal.* Yet he could not shake the overwhelming sense of uncertainty about what had happened earlier when he read that journal. For a moment, he thought he might lose his spaghetti, but he was able to calm himself enough to sit down in front of the old, leather-bound book. There had to be a simple explanation to whatever it was he had experienced earlier today—and besides, when he really stopped to think about it, it had been pretty cool, after all.

Cody took a deep breath and used his index finger to peruse the page and find where he had left off. "There. Blackbeard's death. That is where I stopped," he whispered nervously. With all the determination he could muster, Cody began to read on.

It was early the next morning, still dark outside, when I felt someone's hand on my shoulder, giving me a nudge. . . .

As Cody read these words on the yellowing page, he realized it was happening again. He felt the swimming sensation in his head, the roller-coaster butterflies in his stomach, and the dark spinning mine shaft, all just like it happened earlier. This definitely was no dream, and it must not be a hallucination, either. The next thing he knew, Cody's eyes were fluttering open, and he felt a hand gently nudging his shoulder to wake him. "Edward, son, get up.

We need to be gettin' after some game. Come now, I have our guns ready. Get dressed and let's go," said Edward Sr.

Even though he had just been wide awake in his bedroom, Cody now felt the extreme grogginess of being jostled awake in the pre-dawn darkness. He sat up in his bed, noticing it had a strange feel. The mattress was soft and saggy, as though it was a huge pillowcase stuffed with straw. He swung his legs over the edge of the bed and his feet found the floor. He looked under the bed and saw that his impression of his mattress appeared to be accurate. The mattress was sitting on top of a bed frame that had ropes criss-crossed and stretched tightly to act as a net to hold the mattress. *This would take some getting used to*, thought Cody.

Still groggy, Cody tried to make sense of what was happening. Edward Sr. had said something about going after game. What game? *Oh, yes*, thought Cody, *the deer hunt*. Remembering that Edward Sr. had told his son they would be going after a deer to replenish the family's meat supplies helped snap Cody awake and filled him with excitement. *Maybe I will finally get to shoot a deer*, Cody thought, but then he wondered if that would actually count, since it was in this fantasy world, or whatever this place was.

Edward Sr. had laid some clothes on the foot of the bed for his son to put on. "Where is the camo?" Cody asked.

Edward Sr. looked puzzled. "What do you mean?"

"Camouflage clothes," replied Cody. "We aren't just wearing our normal work clothes, are we?"

"Son, you must still be sleepin', for yer talkin' plumb nonsense!" replied Edward Sr.

Cody realized that hunters in this time must not have worn camouflage clothing. He decided he had better drop it. "Yeah, I guess I must have been having a strange dream when you woke me up," he replied.

"It must've been a whopper. I've never heard ye spout such gibberish!" replied Edward Sr. as he grabbed up two long rifles and headed out to the front porch. Cody quickly got dressed and joined him.

"Looks like it's goin' to be a fine mornin' fer a hunt," said Edward Sr. "With this west wind, I believe we'd be better off goin' over near the spring and sittin' up on the little rock ledge that looks out to the west. The deer always come around there this time of year, and the wind will be in our faces and the sun at our backs. I'll wager we won't have to sit too long this mornin'."

"Sounds good," replied Cody. Edward Sr. led the way, and Cody tried hard to stay right in his tracks. He was impressed at how silently the large man could move through the woods. Edward Sr. seemed to be able to feel his way through the darkness of the early morning. The sandy ground helped to reduce the noise of their footfalls. They had walked in near silence for about ten minutes when Edward Sr. stopped. He turned and motioned for Cody to sit next to him on top of a sand dune that rose gently on one side and then dropped steeply for about twenty feet. Looking down from this height at the moonlit forest floor reminded Cody of the other time he had gone deer hunting, only then he had been sitting on a seat mounted atop a ladder stand, not on a sand dune.

The eastern sky at their backs was beginning to brighten, and the once-brilliant stars of the night sky were starting to fade. Cody watched as the sky changed from black to grey to a brilliant pink as the birds began to fill the silence with their morning songs.

It was still too dark to make out many details on the ground around them, but Cody could see the glimmer from the spring that sat at the base of this small rise. Occasionally, they could hear animals walking nearby. Cody gripped his rifle and waited in nervous anticipation. He had wanted to bag his first deer since the first time he sat in a deer stand. He wondered if he would be up to the challenge if the moment presented itself. He didn't want to fail in front of Edward Sr. He quickly tried to forget his own father's warning about buck fever, the ailment that attacks some hunters right at the moment of truth and makes it nearly impossible for them to hold their weapon steady enough to shoot.

After about twenty minutes of sitting in the exhilarating chill of the early morning, there was finally enough light to make shooting a possibility. Edward Sr. leaned in and whispered to Cody, "Steady now. Deer should be movin' toward their beddin' areas. Let's stay real still. Remember what I taught ye. Scan with your eyes, not your head."

Cody was on full alert. He felt that all of his senses were in tune with his surroundings, yet he wondered how long he would be able to hold this together. He didn't have to wait much longer. Within five minutes of Edward Sr.'s coaching, Cody heard the snapping of a twig come from his right. He tightened his grip on his rifle and very slowly looked in that direction. He didn't see anything at first, but after a moment he saw a flicker of movement as a fine young eight-point buck stepped seemingly out of nowhere. The animal seemed relaxed and unaware of their presence, and he was headed right for them. Cody felt his heart rate quicken and a surge of adrenaline rush through his system.

It was all he could do to keep from jumping out of his skin, but he knew he must try to keep his movements imperceptible. The buck had made its way over to the spring just fifteen yards in front of Cody. When the animal lowered its head to take a drink from the spring, Cody realized that it was his opportunity to raise the rifle and take aim. As he raised the weapon, Cody was afraid that his thumping heartbeat must be so loud that it would surely frighten the deer away. He had never experienced such a rush of energy and emotion. Somehow he was able to calm himself. Just at that moment, he remembered a phrase his grandfather had taught him the first time he ever shot a rifle—

"Aim small, miss small," Cody whispered.

He looked down the long barrel of the gun and placed the little bead at the end right behind the buck's front shoulder. He let out a deep breath and gently squeezed the trigger, just the way his own father had taught him to shoot. *SHHPOWWW!* Cody heard the gun blast, but he couldn't see anything. He had been temporarily blinded by a brilliant flash of gunpowder right in front of his face and the resulting cloud of thick white smoke. That was the one thing Cody had not been prepared for. He was shooting a flintlock rifle, not a modern gun. He quickly shook off the shock and blindness and tried to see what the result of his shot had been. He heard the deer bound off in the same direction from which it had come. Had he hit the mark or missed? Edward Sr. quickly relieved his apprehension.

"Good shot, my boy. He won't be goin' far." Even as he heard these words, Cody could hear the buck crash about forty yards away.

He had done it! He had killed his first deer, and it was an eight-pointer at that! Then he came to the sobering realization that he would not have a trophy to show for his efforts. *I finally kill a buck and I can't even show it to anyone!* he thought. *Oh, well. Maybe the experience will help me when I hunt again for real.*

Cody and Edward Sr. worked their way down the little rise and went after the fallen buck. As they approached the animal, Cody was flooded with a combination of pride, excitement, and sadness. He had not been prepared for the overwhelming emotional experience of the taking of life from such a large and marvelous animal. He began to shake uncontrollably.

Edward Sr. couldn't help but notice what the boy was going through and attempted to comfort him. "It is a powerful thing, isn't it, son? I know just what yer feelin'. You feel good, sad, and pert' near everything in between. Well, son, that's what a hunter should feel. The good Lord put the beasts of the field out here for our benefit. They are beautiful and noble animals. They provide for us and help to sustain us. We should respect them for offerin' up their lives for us," Edward Sr. said as he gently put his hand on Cody's shoulder. "Indian folks say prayers to honor the spirits of the game they kill. I don't know if that buck has a spirit, but I always feel like we owe them some respect. That's why it is right'n proper fer you to feel the way you do now. I still feel it, too, and I've been doin' this fer a long time."

Edward Sr.'s words made good sense, and Cody began to calm down. He was glad to understand his mixed emotions, and he hoped he would feel that way again whenever he had a successful hunt. It was a good sort of feeling, almost like getting to know a part of you that you didn't even know existed—an ancient part of you somehow connected to all of history.

"We better get to work. This job ain't gonna do itself," said Edward Sr. as he bent over the fallen buck and reached for the knife sheath strapped to his leg. He opened the sheath and pulled out the knife. It was no ordinary knife, but a beautifully crafted work of art. The fixed blade was about four inches long, and the handle was a little bit longer and very thick. The eye-catching handle appeared to be made of bone or perhaps antler. It was intricately carved with delicate images of deer, elk, buffalo, and bears. Cody had never seen a knife like this.

"Did you make that knife, Pa?" he asked.

"Good heavens, no," Edward Sr. replied. He paused. "Have I never told you the story of this knife?"

"Not that I can remember," Cody replied.

"Well, after we get back to the house and bone out this meat, I will tell it to you," promised Edward Sr. "You might want to put that story in yer journal, too."

When the job of preparing the deer was complete and they had returned to the Carter house, Edward Sr. and Cody sat on the front porch. As Cody looked out at the nearby town of Beaufort imagining what it must have looked like to see the *Queen Anne's Revenge* stuck on a sandbar out in the channel, Edward Sr., having just lit his pipe, reached again for the knife strapped to his leg. He inspected the tool closely to make sure that he had sufficiently cleaned it and then handed it to Cody for closer inspection.

"You know, to this very day, I still don't know who made that knife or even where it comes from," Edward Sr. said. "But I can tell you the story of when I found it and why I keep it—if, that is, yer of a mind to hear it."

"Sure I am," said Cody, eagerly.

"I've been savin' this story for a long time now, 'cause it ain't the most pleasant story to tell, or hear. I guess yer old enough now that yer ready to hear it—after all, I was a bit younger than you are now when I lived through it," said Edward Sr.

This sounds promising, thought Cody, as he settled himself in and braced himself for whatever he was about to hear.

Edward Sr. took a deep draw from his pipe, sat back, blew out a long stream of pungent tobacco smoke, and began to speak.

"Our family hasn't always lived here in Beaufort, ye know. My parents came down into North Carolina from Virginia Colony about 1710, when I was just a lad of about twelve. My father built a fine farm near the mouth of the Neuse River, a few miles north of New Bern, which had been founded by some Swiss and German settlers. A whole lot of folks were comin' down into North Carolina in those times 'cause Virginia was startin' to get a little crowded for some people's tastes. My pa had as fine a tobacco farm as you ever saw, I reckon. He raised a little corn and indigo, too. He worked awful hard and 'course, he had a few slaves to help him. I was still a little bit too small to be much of a farmhand. I've never owned any slaves myself. I just can't hardly justify it in my head to own another human bein'. But I can sure understand why some men, like my Pa, had 'em. A feller just can't hardly compete with other farms if they have to pay their labor while others have slave labor for free."

Cody had not known for sure that his family had once owned slaves, though he had suspected that it was a real possibility since his family had come from the South. He found some comfort in the fact that at least Edward Sr. had taken a stand against owning slaves of his own.

"Anyhow," Edward Sr. continued, "Pa had built up a fine farm. He had a little over three hundred acres with some fine bottom land and a big plantation house. Our future looked mighty bright—until the awful Tuscarora War."

Cody quickly scanned his memory, but could not recall ever learning anything about an event by this name.

"What was the Tuscarora War, Pa?" Cody asked.

"It was in that dark year of 1711," Edward Sr. replied. "North Carolina Colony wasn't very strong. In fact, there was a whole mess of political squabblin' goin' on about who was the rightful governor. People took sides and were fightin' against one another. The town of New Bern had been built over the site of an old Indian town called Cartouca, and in 1711 the Indians decided they wanted it back. The man who had surveyed the site of the town of New

Men at work in a tobacco field in Watauga County, North Carolina, in the 1950s. The tobacco field that belonged to Edward Carter Jr.'s grandfather may have been similar.

Bern was named John Lawson. He was lookin' to expand the region and open it up for more white settlers comin' down from Virginia. The Tuscarora Indians saw this as a big threat to their huntin' grounds, and they didn't like it one bit. I can't say as I can blame 'em, really. It seems like the Indians have been gettin' pushed out of their lands every time the white settlers take a notion to spread out some more. I'll tell you, son, I have known a few Indian folks in my time, and some of 'em are as fine a people as you'll ever meet, but you don't want to make an enemy out of 'em. Some of the things I saw Indian warriors do keep me up nights all these years later," said Edward Sr. with a slight tremble in his voice.

He paused to relight his pipe and shift positions in his chair. Cody could sense a little uneasiness in the man, as if he dreaded telling the rest of the story. Edward Sr. cleared his throat and resumed his tale.

"I've told ye of course, that yer grandparents died when I was thirteen years old. Well, this here is the story of how that happened. I didn't want you to hear it 'til I was sure you were old enough to handle it, and I reckon today is that day. The Indians captured that Lawson feller and another man that he was showin' some land to up the Neuse River. They executed Lawson, and the stories spread of how gruesome they did it. They say they burned him alive, real slow like . . . drawin' it out as long as they could. It makes my stomach turn to think of it. I don't know if it is true or not, but that is the story that went around. The Indian chief in these parts was called King Hancock. He organized all the local tribes to go on the warpath against the white settlements and take back their land. Hancock gathered up most of the Indians in the lands between the Neuse and Pamlico Rivers . . . the Coree, Matchapunga, Pamlico, Bear River, and Neusioc Indians were among them. They struck their blow at sunrise on September 22, 1711. That is the date that is etched into the grave markers of my parents, and you and I are both lucky that my own tombstone isn't right alongside of theirs. When it happened, my ma was fixin' breakfast, and my pa was out gettin' a team of horses ready for workin'. I was awake, but still lyin' in my bed. I can still remember smellin' the bacon Ma was cookin' when I heard the commotion outside. That bacon smell is one of my last memories of my parents alive, and I still think of 'em whenever I smell bacon fryin' to this very day."

Edward Sr. seemed now to be almost in a trance. His eyes appeared glazed over. Cody got the impression that he had shifted into autopilot just to be able to get through this story.

Edward Sr. resumed his grisly tale.

"When I heard the ruckus the horses were makin', I bolted up from bed and looked out the window. I saw Pa spin around to face an oncomin' Indian. I saw the Indian raise his rifle and fire, and I saw my pa crumple to the ground. I don't think Pa ever knew what hit him. Then I saw the Indian take out a knife and grab Pa by the hair, and I turned away. I didn't want to see what he was goin' to do, but I knew he was about to scalp my pa. I am just glad he wasn't alive fer it—some folks weren't so lucky. The other Indians in the war party set fire to the barn and outbuildings, and then I saw them headin' fer the house. My ma had run outside with one of Pa's rifles. I saw her blast one of the Indians as they were approachin' the porch, but there were just too many, and they overran her. I knew there wasn't a thing in the world fer me to do to help, so I did the only reasonable thing left to do: I ran fer my very life. I went through the back door and ran as fast as I could go. It was about three miles into New Bern, and I knew it would be the safest place fer me. When I made it to the town, I saw there were a lot of other people there at the little fortification that was built fer just such an occasion. Some of the folks that gathered were townsfolk, and some were from the surroundin' farms like me. We learned

This image is reputed to be of John Lawson (1674–1711), explorer and surveyor, who helped lay out the towns of Bath and New Bern in North Carolina. In 1711 he was captured and executed by the Tuscarora Indians.

later that there were many small Indian war parties like the one that hit our farm all up and down the Neuse and Pamlico Valleys. The attacks lasted only about two hours but left 130 dead colonists in their wake. The stories of the attacks were heart wrenchin'. Some of the settlers had been tortured horribly. Many of the dead bodies had been desecrated. The less fortunate ones had been taken captive, and God only knows what happened to them. The rest, like myself, ran for their lives, leavin' the bodies of their loved ones at the mercy of the savages or the scavengers."

Cody's heart ached at hearing these words. He had read accounts of Indian wars in books, but they never truly seemed real until now. Here was a member of his own family who had witnessed atrocities that probably were unimaginable to anyone living in Cody's time. Cody felt the need to say something comforting to Edward Sr., but nothing seemed to come to mind. The only thing he could think to say came out before he had time to stop it.

"So where does the knife come in?" Cody asked, worried that it seemed too trivial in light of the heavy story he had just been told.

"Ah yes, the knife," replied Edward Sr. "Well, we all stayed pretty close to New Bern for a day or so. When it seemed safe to venture out, some of the men decided to make a sweep of the surroundin' homesteads to search for survivors, bury the dead, and salvage anything that could be saved. I went along with a family friend by the name of Martin Mackenzie. He helped me rummage through what was left of my parents' place. It pains me considerable even now to recollect the images of my parents' bodies as we cleaned them up and made them as presentable as we could. We gave 'em a Christian burial on a lovely spot overlookin' the Neuse River a few hundred yards east of the burned-out house. We returned to the home site and started lookin' through the rubble for anything that might be salvaged. There wasn't much of anything left. The only thing I found worth pickin' up was this here knife. I don't know whose it was. I know it wasn't my pa's. I reckon it was dropped by one of the Indians. I didn't rightly know if it was Indian made or if it was somethin' they had plundered off of another farm somewhere. I really didn't care. I only knew that it was all I had left to show fer the farm my parents had built together. I have kept it ever since as a reminder of all that was taken from me on that bloody day."

Edward Sr. appeared to be spent from reliving those terrible events from his childhood. Cody handed the knife back to him as he finished his tale.

"My parents' land and slaves were sold to pay off debts. I went back to Virginia to live with my uncle William. I didn't return to North Carolina until after I married yer ma when I was seventeen. We came down here to Beaufort, and you were born about a year later," said Edward Sr.

As soon as Edward Sr. had finished speaking, Cody felt light headed, and a curtain seemed to open in front of him again. Everything went black for a moment, and then he found himself back in his own bedroom. He felt very tired and very sad.

PART TWO

The Journal of Ethan Carter
Yadkin Valley Settlements, North Carolina, 1757

3

At least Cody was now certain of something: What had been happening to him while reading the journal of Edward Carter was certainly no dream. It had now happened more than once, and he had experienced the same sensations each time. But there were still lots of unanswered questions swirling in Cody's head. Was the Edward Carter journal the only one that was *magic?* Would he go through this when he read some of the other journals, too? He knew there was only one way to find out. He set aside Edward's journal and looked into the box to find another. Cody always liked to do things in the correct order, so he had already planned to go through the journals chronologically. The next book in the time line was labeled *The Journal of Ethan Carter 1757*. He sat the old book, which looked very similar to Edward's journal, on his desk. He decided he didn't quite feel up to starting it just now. "I will look at you tomorrow after church," Cody said, staring at the journal.

Sunday morning found Cody sitting in a church pew making a weak attempt to listen to the sermon. He heard just enough of it to realize that it was something about forgiveness, but he simply had too much on his mind to concentrate properly. All night he had tossed and turned, dreaming about the journal. He was both looking forward to opening it and dreading it at the same time. So many unanswered questions continued to eat away at him. He had other worries besides whether the journals would transport him back in time. He thought about his experiences in Edward Carter's journal, recalling the horrible events of the Indian attacks on Neuse River settlements. That story had been told through young Edward's father, so Cody didn't actually have to witness the horror firsthand. But he himself had experienced splitting wood and actually felt the strain and soreness from that work. He also remembered the emotional whirlwind of the deer hunt. That experience had been vividly real. What if he had actually experienced the Indian raid? How could he handle an experience like that? He realized that if he was transported into any more journals, he would have to be prepared for the possibility that he might experience something very traumatic. Still, he felt an exhilarating rush of anticipation at what adventures could be awaiting him.

Later that afternoon, Cody headed up to his bedroom. He sat down at his desk and stared for a few long seconds at the old journal in front of him. "Well, here goes nothing," he mumbled. He took a deep breath and reached for the book. He opened it to the first page and began to read.

> *January 20th 1757 My name is Ethan Carter. I am fifteen years of age.*
> *I am living in the Bryan Camp on the Yadkin River in the colony of North*
> *Carolina. I have been here in this settlement for a little more than three*
> *months now. I've been orphaned for the last four months. In the last year*
> *I have lost both my parents to the consumption. I took the money from the*
> *sale of my parents' estate and traveled south from Virginia with a company*
> *of other settlers led here by Mr. Morgan Bryan. I purchased fifty acres of*
> *bottom land here along the Yadkin River. Though I live mostly by myself, I*
> *have been fortunate to have a couple nearby that looks in on me from time to*
> *time. Their names are Daniel and Rebecca Boone. They are but a few years*
> *my senior, but they have taken it on themselves as a newly married couple to*
> *see that I am doing alright. I am old enough to take care of myself, but truth*
> *be told, I am glad they have taken an interest in me. . . .*

Cody had gotten quite a bit further into the reading than he had in the previous journal, and he had just allowed himself to think it must be a regular book when his head began to swim and he felt the butterflies in his stomach. Everything went dark for a moment and seemed to spin.

When Cody opened his eyes again, he found himself in a partially cleared field with an axe in his hand. He was standing in front of a beech tree that was about halfway chopped through. "Again, with an axe?" Cody moaned. It was pretty cold outside—Cody guessed somewhere in the mid-thirties—but he was sweating. As he looked around the clearing, he saw that this axe had been quite busy. There was a mostly level patch of ground full of tree stumps about a foot high. The width of the clearing ran from the river to Cody's right, across a level field for about 150 yards to a small wooded hill on his left. The length ran at least 300 yards out in front of him, cluttered with stumps all the way. At the end of the clearing, at the foot of another small wooded hillside, was a pitiful-looking log cabin.

Cody decided to go back to chopping the tree in front of him. He got a good grip on the axe handle, took aim at the tree, brought the axe back, and put his weight behind a mighty swing . . . *SHWAAACKK* . . . the axe found its mark and knocked a large chip out of the growing crevasse in the trunk of the beech. As he was about to swing again, Cody thought he heard something. He stood still and listened. "Hey, Ethan!" came a faint voice from the direction of the little cabin at the end of the field.

So, I am Ethan Carter this time, Cody thought.

"Ethan Carter!" the voice said, just a touch louder and clearer this time. Cody squinted up toward the cabin and saw a man walking down the hillside.

"I'm out here in the field clearin' trees!" Cody shouted. As he trudged through the stump-stubbled field toward the man, Cody took inventory of his situation. He noticed that he felt much bigger than normal. He glanced down at himself and saw he was wearing similar clothing to what Edward Carter had worn, only a little dirtier and more worn out. He looked down at his arms, and he sensed that he had some pretty impressive muscles working under his shirt sleeves. When he got to within about fifty feet of the little cabin, the man spoke again.

"Rebecca and I are plannin' on makin' syrup tomorrow, Ethan. We were wonderin' if you would be interested in coming to help. You can have your share of it if you want to help," he said.

Cody took a good look at the man in front of him. He was a very impressive-looking person . . . average height, powerfully built, with an air of importance. He appeared to be in his early twenties. He was wearing buckskins and carried a long rifle. In fact, he looked an awful lot like the images Cody had seen of the famous Daniel Boone, but that seemed impossible. Cody searched his memory for anything he might have learned about Daniel Boone in school or in books. Wasn't Boone married to a woman named Rebecca? That sounded about right. Didn't he live in North Carolina for a while? It seemed like that was right, too. Cody remembered that Boone had led the settlers through the Cumberland Gap into Kentucky in 1775. That would be in another eighteen years from this time, and this Daniel Boone would be in his mid-forties by then. That seemed about right, too. If this wasn't *the* Daniel Boone, he was doing an awfully good impression.

Daniel was waiting for Cody's answer. "I wouldn't miss it," replied Cody.

"Well, that's fine, Ethan. Why don't you just come on back with me and have supper with us tonight? You can stay with us, and we'll get an early start on it tomorrow," said the man.

TENNESSEE STATE LIBRARY AND ARCHIVES

Daniel Boone (1734–1820) shown sitting on a cliff edge, holding a rifle. The image is meant to depict Boone's first sighting of Kentucky in 1769.

"Sounds real good," replied Cody.

"I can wait right here fer you if you want to clean up a bit," Daniel said.

Cody thought that sounded like a good idea, and he walked inside the cabin. *This must be where Ethan lives*, he thought. The little shelter was barely a shelter at all. The walls were only about five feet high and made of rough-cut logs. Cody suspected that the logs had once been on top of some of those stumps out in the field. There appeared to be mud chinking between the logs, but the logs were not hewn flat and were very uneven. Light could be seen pouring in through cracks all throughout the tiny one-room building. The cabin's floor was just hard-packed dirt. There was a fire pit at one end of the room, and a small fire was smoldering in it. The smoke from the fire was escaping through a hole in the roof directly over the fire pit. The roof had a slight pitch, so that the indoor ceiling was high enough for Cody to stand up straight, but only in the middle of the room. On the wall opposite the fire pit was a small bed that looked similar to Edward Carter's bed, only not as big and not nearly as clean. A small table with a few kitchen items on it stood against the back wall. There was a tin cup and plate, a pitcher full of water, some salt, and what appeared to be some sort of jerky hanging from the wall. Cody looked around for a moment. "That tour didn't take long," he whispered to himself. He guessed the size of the cabin to be twelve feet long and eight feet wide.

Nothing in the room resembled a dresser, but Cody spotted a large wooden box. He lifted the lid and pulled out a set of buckskins that looked similar to the ones Daniel was wearing. He pulled off his dirty, sweat-soaked clothing and walked over to the pitcher of water. He poured some water from the pitcher into his cupped hand and splashed it over himself. He splashed some more water and rubbed some of the dirt and sweat off of his skin. He noticed that he smelled a little gamey. He pulled on the buckskin pants, a fresh white shirt, and a buckskin jacket. As he did so, a small, leather-bound book almost tumbled out of the jacket's pocket. Cody retrieved it, then wrestled on a pair of long boots made of some sort of animal hide, probably deer, he guessed. He then took what was left of water in the pitcher and tossed it onto the fire. Most of the flames went out immediately, and smoke began to fill the room. He kicked a couple sticks of wood around to spread them out so they wouldn't blaze back up. Satisfied that the fire was out for good, he stepped outside.

"We'd better get steppin' if we're gonna make it to Sugartree Creek before dark," said Daniel.

The two headed over the little hill behind Ethan's cabin and followed a well-worn trail through the woods. They were following the river that ran beside the cabin and field where Cody had first been standing. "The Yadkin is flowin' pretty heavy. There must have been some snowmelt up in the high country in the last couple days. Spring won't be too far off now," Daniel said.

Cody knew from the journal that Ethan's land sat along the Yadkin River. He assumed from what the man had said that the Boones' cabin must be on a creek that fed the Yadkin—Sugartree Creek, he had called it. As the two continued walking, Daniel spoke again. "I'm aimin' to take one more hunting trip before spring. I'm goin' to go up into the high country, up around the headwaters of the Yadkin. I could use some company if you've a mind to go along."

"I would love to go," replied Cody.

"Fine then. Let's plan on leavin' in about five days. We'll be gone fer a couple weeks at least, so plan accordingly."

Cody began to lose all sense of time as his head whirled with excitement. *Am I really going on a hunting trip with Daniel Boone?* he kept repeating in his mind. After about twenty minutes of walking, the two veered off the course of the river and followed another trail that ran along a small tributary creek. Cody assumed it must be Sugartree Creek. Another five minutes' hike brought them to a clearing and a cabin. Out of the door of the cabin stepped a very lovely young woman. She was tall, nearly as tall as Daniel, with fair skin, black

The Daniel Boone Memorial Cabin in Davidson County, North Carolina, was built in 1910. Daniel and Rebecca Boone's cabin on Sugartree Creek would have looked a lot like this one.

hair, and striking dark eyes. She appeared to be a bit younger than Daniel, probably still in her teens, Cody guessed. He also noticed that her belly protruded slightly under her apron, and Cody wondered if she was expecting a baby. *This must be Rebecca*, he thought.

"Howdy, Ethan. Hello, Daniel," the young woman said.

"Hello, Rebecca," Cody replied. His excitement grew. Surely this was THE Daniel Boone!

"How are things over on the Yadkin?" asked Rebecca.

"I'm close to gettin' a field cleared," Cody answered.

"Come on in the house. I've got supper nearly ready," Rebecca said.

The three of them sat down to a table of bear meat, potatoes, turnips, and bread. Cody had never tried bear meat and he hated turnips, but he took heaping helpings of everything and devoured it all. He found it all to be very tasty and satisfying.

After supper, Cody sat in the main room of the cabin with Daniel. He looked around at his surroundings. *Now this*, he thought, *was a real cabin*. It was much bigger than Ethan Carter's place, about eighteen feet by twenty-four feet. It had a separate room for cooking and dining. It had a proper fireplace with a stone chimney. There was a large main room with a bed along the back wall. The biggest improvements of this cabin were the walls and the floor. Unlike Ethan, Boone had taken the trouble to hew his logs flat so that they fit together snugly. This made for a much less drafty living space. He also had added a wooden floor. *I'll dread going back to the other cabin after this*, Cody thought.

"So, Ethan," Boone began, "I want to get one more huntin' trip in before spring, before the baby's born in May or thereabouts. I'll hate to leave Rebecca alone with a newborn. I'm glad you decided to go with me on the trip. I think you'll like it. You've never been up in the high country yet, have you?"

"No, I haven't, but I hear it's awful pretty in the Blue Ridge," Cody replied.

"Oh, it's a magical place, Ethan. I've got an itch to go out past the Blue Ridge and into the land of *Cain-tuck-ee*. Indians and fur traders say it's a real Eden over there. I'm gonna go one day. There's gettin' to be too many folks 'round these parts. The west is callin' to me. I can just hear it. Maybe you'll go with me and see fer yourself one of these days," said Daniel.

"Maybe I just will," Cody answered.

"As fer the syrup," Daniel said, "I've checked some of the buckets hangin' on the trees nearest the house here, and there's a right smart of sap flowin'. I reckon we should have all we want and then some."

After a bit more small talk, Rebecca suggested that they all turn in. "We have a big day ahead tomorrow. Best be well rested," she said. She laid out a pallet for Ethan to sleep on fairly close to the fireplace, then she and Daniel retired to the bed along the back wall. As he sat in the flickering firelight, Cody remembered the little leather-bound book and wondered whether it was Ethan's journal. He pulled it out of his jacket pocket, but he'd no sooner begun to open it when he sensed a curtain opening before him. He felt the swimming sensation in his head and the butterflies in his gut. Just as he began to black out, his head jerked up, and he opened his eyes to his own bedroom.

4

Cody was really excited now. He was almost certain that he had just met someone really famous. "That must have been THE Daniel Boone," he said to himself, in an attempt to make it sound official. But there was a way to make doubly sure. He opened up the Internet browser on his computer and typed "Daniel Boone" into a search engine. He found a website that gave a lot of information on Boone's early life and clicked on the link. Cody scanned through the information to confirm what he had recalled earlier. Boone was born in Pennsylvania in 1734. Cody quickly did the math in his head. He estimated the Daniel Boone he met to be in his early twenties, and THE Daniel Boone would have been about twenty-three in 1757. Check. Boone moved to the Yadkin Valley with his parents in 1751. Check. He married Rebecca Bryan in 1756. Check. Their first son, James, was born on May 3, 1757. Check. And there it was. Everything checked out.

"A member of my family was friends with Daniel Boone!" Cody said to himself proudly. "And I got to meet him, too!" Suddenly he was struck with a strange notion. He had just read about some things that the young Daniel Boone didn't know yet. He knew the exact date when the Boones' first child was to be born. He knew that it would be a boy. He even knew the baby's name. This made Cody a little apprehensive. *I had better be careful if I go back with that journal again. I better not slip up and reveal information that I shouldn't,* he thought. To be sure, Cody decided he would be better off not researching any further ahead about Daniel Boone's life in the Yadkin Valley. He would just see where the journal took him.

When he arrived home after school on Monday, Cody headed straight for his room. He found his place in the journal of Ethan Carter and began to read.

We were up before first light the next morning. Rebecca had made a pot of coffee and some biscuits. After a quick breakfast of salt pork and biscuits, we headed out for a day of syrup making. I had never done this before and I was looking forward to it. . . .

As Cody read, he began to feel the same sensations that had pulled him into the journal before. When he opened his eyes this time, he found himself outside the Boones' cabin, standing with Daniel in the predawn light. "Well, Ethan," said Daniel, "we might just as well get started. We have a lot of ground to cover and a lot of sap to haul back here. You say you've never made syrup before?"

"That's right. Sure like eating it, though," Cody responded.

"Well, we've had our trees tapped fer over a month now, and the sap's been runnin' right heavy since the warm-up after the last hard freeze. We have a heap of sugar maples all along through these parts—that's why this here creek is called Sugartree. We went out and drilled little holes in some of the best trees, and then we drove spiles into the holes. Spiles are like little spigots. They let the sap drain out. Then we hung little buckets off the spiles and have waited a few weeks for the sap to run into those buckets. Now you and me have to go out and fetch those buckets and bring 'em back here to Rebecca. She'll boil

These sap buckets are much like those Ethan Carter would have worked with when he and Boone collected sap for syrup making, although the buckets likely would have been made from wood.

down the sap, and that will leave us with the syrup. It's mighty good, as you already know. It's about the only thing we have out here to sweeten with. Hardly any sugar available, and most can't afford it anyhow," Daniel replied.

"How many buckets will we collect?" asked Cody.

"Best I recollect, we tapped about 120 trees. It takes a right smart of sap to make much syrup. About thirty or forty gallons of sap will make one gallon of syrup—it boils down to pert' near nothin' by the time it's done," Daniel replied.

"Seems like an awful lot of trouble for such a little yield," Cody said.

"The way I look at it, Ethan, is sometimes you either have to do, or you do without." Boone replied.

"I guess that's so," said Cody. "Let's get a move on."

The two began the tedious task of gathering bucket after bucket of the thick, sweet-smelling sap. They had a long skinny pole with notches cut in it, and each would carry one end. Each bucket they retrieved would be hung from the pole, allowing them to carry a few buckets at a time. When they had a full load, the weight of the buckets would strain the hickory pole to its limit. They then would return to a little outbuilding near the Boones' cabin. Daniel called this their sugarhouse. There Rebecca began the process of boiling the sap. "You have to boil all the water out of the sap before you can get syrup," she explained.

It was hot work in the sugarhouse. Rebecca was wearing a full-length dress and a cap, but she did allow herself the luxury of rolling up her sleeves a bit. Her right sleeve was stained dark from where she had been constantly wiping the sweat from her brow. The fire in the little shack had to be maintained and kept extremely hot to do the job. After the third trip back to the sugarhouse, Cody finally saw a glass jug with some of the finished product in it. It was a dark, amber-colored syrup, and it looked and smelled delicious.

"I see you're eyeballin' the syrup there, Ethan. Want to sample a spoonful?" asked Rebecca.

"Sure," answered Cody. Rebecca dipped a small wooden spoon into the mouth of the jug and pulled up a dollop of its gooey contents. She handed the spoon to Cody, and he touched it to his lips. He let the thick, viscous liquid slowly spread across his taste buds. It was heavenly—the best-tasting syrup Cody had ever had, perhaps because he had a lot of sweat equity invested in the process. He felt a sense of accomplishment unlike anything he had ever experienced. *It is really cool*, Cody thought, *to make your own food from scratch*. He remembered the similar feelings he had experienced after harvesting the deer

Daniel Boone's rifle was carved with images of Native Americans, nature, and animals as well as his name.

to help provide table fare for Edward Carter's family. He realized how things are much more special when you have to work hard for them. It was a good feeling. "This is delicious, Rebecca," Cody said.

"Just be careful not to rub any on your forehead, or your tongue will slap your brains out tryin' to get at it!" joked Rebecca.

Laughing, Cody and Daniel headed back out to finish retrieving the rest of the sap buckets. The job of sap retrieval took most of the day, and the evaporating work went on into the evening. By the end of the day, the Boones and Cody had boiled off more than three gallons of maple syrup. They were all tired and ready for a meal and some relaxation.

After supper, Daniel and Cody retired to the porch and began planning their upcoming trip. "You've said you've never been up in the Blue Ridge yet, Ethan," Daniel began. "I can tell you that it is a place of wonder. You can feel spirits in the Blue Ridge. It is Cherokee country, and you can just feel it in your bones. Those mountains do somethin' to a man. We'll be followin' the Yadkin right up to its source. There's a place there called the Blowing Rock—spirits are real heavy in the air there. It'll plumb near make your flesh crawl—beautiful place, but there's a darkness about it. I'll tell you what the Indians say about it when we get there," Daniel said. "Wouldn't do any good to tell you about it now. You'll just have to *feel* it fer yourself."

"How long will we be gone?" Cody asked.

"Oh, two or three weeks, maybe more, maybe less—all depends on what we run into. If there's plenty of game about, we may be gone a bit longer—if there's any hostile Cherokee about, we may need to scoot outta there a little quicker. I've gotten along pretty well with the Cherokee most of the time, but I never totally trust 'em. We'll need to take along plenty of trade goods to keep 'em on our good side. We just have to remember to always be alert when we travel in the Blue Ridge," answered Daniel.

Cody was a little uneasy. This sounded a little scary, dangerous even. He felt a little stirring in his gut. Suddenly he felt lightheaded, and everything seemed to be going dark. When he opened his eyes, he was back in his room. He sat for a long moment staring at the old journal. He was having second thoughts about whether to finish reading this or not.

"Hostiles ... spirits ... darkness. I'm not sure I like the sounds of that," Cody moaned.

5

Cody stared at Ethan Carter's journal with apprehension. He was unsure whether he should read on. He knew that traveling into the wilderness of the Blue Ridge Mountains with Daniel Boone was an opportunity for adventure that he would never have imagined, but there were many unknown dangers. Cody had sensed that even Boone had seemed a little nervous about the high country. That is what really worried him.

Cody decided he needed to do some research about this area and this time period before he made his decision. He went to his computer and searched about North Carolina in the late 1750s. What he learned, at first, did not ease his concerns. It was during the years of the French and Indian War. Cody remembered a little bit about the war from history class. He knew that the war was fought between the French and the British for control of lands on the western frontier of the British colonies in America. He remembered that various Indian tribes had taken sides with either the French or the British and joined in the fighting. Cody now learned that the French and Indian War had hit very close to home for the Boones and the other settlers in the Yadkin Valley. By the time Ethan Carter had befriended Boone, Boone had already served a stint under the command of British General Edward Braddock. In fact, Boone had been a part of a major failed campaign of Braddock's troops in the Ohio Country. The year was 1755, and General Braddock was attempting a daring offensive maneuver to drive the French out of the Ohio Valley. They focused their efforts on the French Fort Duquesne along the Monongahela River, on the site of present-day Pittsburgh, Pennsylvania. The British force was aided by some American colonial militia, including a young George Washington. Before they ever had a chance to get to the fort, they were intercepted by a smaller group of French. The ensuing Battle of the Wilderness turned out to be one of the most demoralizing and embarrassing defeats of the British in the seven-year war. The battle was completely one-sided. Of the more than

1,300 British and American troops, nearly 900 were killed or wounded. General Braddock was among those who lost their lives. About fifty women had accompanied the troops as maids and cooks. Of that number, only four survived. Boone and Washington had been among the survivors who were forced to retreat and regroup. The French and their Indian allies, although badly outnumbered at the start of the skirmish, reported only about forty total casualties. "Geez," muttered Cody as he read the account of the battle. "Boone must have seen some horrible things at that battle."

Cody continued to research and soon found that the French and Indian War eventually found its way to the settlements of the Yadkin Valley. In 1759, encouraged by the French, bands of Cherokee attacked the Yadkin settlers. The Cherokee had actually been allies of the British at the beginning of the conflict but felt mistreated and switched their allegiance to the French. With the raids by the Cherokee, most of the Yadkin settlers, including the Boone family, were forced to abandon their homes and flee north into Virginia. "So Ethan met Daniel Boone in between a couple of periods of major drama," Cody said to himself. "I wonder if Ethan got out all right when the Cherokee attacked?"

Cody had learned a great deal from his research, and he paused to let it sink in. He was still considering whether or not he wanted to venture back into Ethan Carter's journal. Finally, he sighed deeply and said with resolve, "I just can't miss this chance to go exploring with Daniel Boone." He turned to face his desk and dragged his index finger along the yellowed old journal page until he found the next entry. He began to read.

I met D. Boone at his cabin just after first light this morning. He had a packhorse loaded down with our provisions. The two of us would walk. . . .

The words on the page began to swim, and this time when Cody emerged from the spinning darkness, he was standing outside the Boone cabin on Sugartree Creek.

"Mornin', Ethan," said Daniel. "Ready to go, I see."

"Been lookin' forward to it," Cody replied.

"We'll make right good time for the first couple days," Daniel answered. "The trail is pretty well worn for a good ways, and the land is mostly flat. We'll get slowed down considerable as we get over 'round the Pilot Mountain and more so beyond that. We'll have t'do some powerful climbin' when we reach the Blue Ridge."

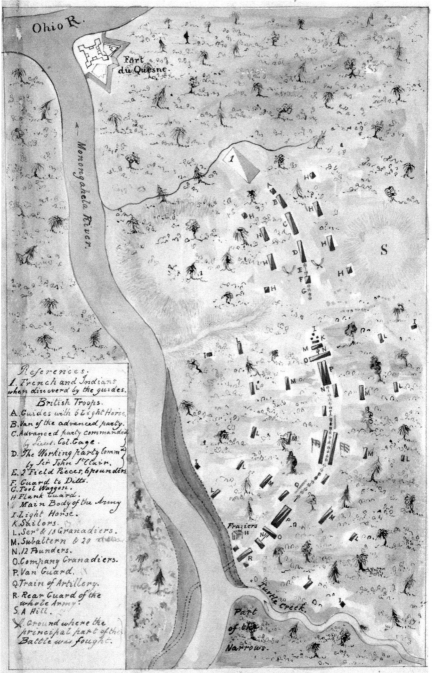

This page from General Braddock's journal depicts where British troops were on the battlefield at the time of the Battle of the Wilderness on July 9, 1755. Various markings on the map indicate the responsibilities of the soldier or group of soldiers in each area, which Braddock explains in his key at the bottom left.

"I'm up for it," replied Cody, who wasn't at all sure if he was as confident as he sounded. The two headed downstream along Sugartree Creek for a short distance until they reached the mouth of the stream as it flowed into the Yadkin River.

"This here is our guide," said Daniel. "The river will take us right to the high country." They followed the river upstream in a generally northward direction. As Daniel had promised, the walking was fairly easy at this point, and they rattled off the miles at a pretty fast clip.

"We won't worry about huntin' much the first day or two. The game is about played out here close to the settlements," said Daniel. "We'll buckle down and start walkin' a little more stealthy-like when we get out aways further."

They walked all morning and afternoon. Cody noticed the land grew progressively hillier as they went along.

By late afternoon they had traveled nearly fifteen miles. Cody's feet were sore and his muscles were tired. Daniel, it seemed, wasn't the least bit tired. They would have made it even further, but then Daniel shot the first deer of the trip. Daniel's skill with a long rifle was amazing—he dropped the large doe in her tracks from nearly a hundred yards away. Watching him handle a skinning knife was like watching an artist paint a masterpiece. Cody was transfixed as Boone deftly removed the doe's hide and scraped, or flensed, the excess fat and tissue from the underside. He then rubbed salt on the hide to help preserve it. "I'm hopin' to come back with thirty or forty bucks on this trip," said Daniel. "They're worth the same as a dollar in cash apiece. That'll buy a lot of provisions, and with a baby comin', Lord knows we could use the money."

Daniel had called deer skins bucks, Cody thought, *and he said they could be used the same as a dollar of cash—that must be why we call a dollar a buck.*

As quick as Daniel had been in completing the work of preparing the deer hide, the task had still used up most of the last hour of daylight. "We best make camp here tonight. We'll be goin' by Pilot Mountain in the morning. That'll give us a good high spot to look out for Indian campfire smoke before we head on further. I haven't had much trouble gettin' along with the Cherokee or the Catawba that live in the high country, but just the same, I'd prefer to know where they are before we run across any of 'em," said Daniel.

"Sounds like a good plan to me," Cody agreed.

Daniel retrieved the bedrolls from the pack horse and spread them out under some hemlock trees. Cody had camped out in tents before, but he had never slept out in the open like this. It had not been a particularly cold day for early February; in fact, walking that distance had actually been quite hot work. Cody estimated the high temperature for the day had been in the mid-fifties, but it was bound to drop off and be pretty chilly at night. Daniel handed Cody a couple of wool blankets and then proceeded to build a fire.

"Ethan, why don't you take my tomahawk and go and cut us a few shelter poles about six or eight feet long?" said Daniel. A little unsure of what to do, Cody took the little hatchet and headed into the woods. He found some sapling trees about an inch or two in diameter and chopped them down. When he had gathered five of these, he headed back to the campsite. "Those'll do fine," said Daniel. Cody watched as Daniel trimmed away the branches of each tree and then cut each tree to a length of about eight feet. He then took several deer hide strips and tied the poles together into a makeshift frame. "Go and cut us some hemlock boughs now," Daniel said.

Now Cody understood what was going on. Daniel was building an open-face shelter for them to sleep under. Cody cut and gathered a couple big armloads of the evergreen hemlock branches and helped Daniel lay them out on the pole frame. When they had finished, they had a three-sided shelter with the opening facing the campfire. With the shelter finished and darkness now enveloping them, Cody and Daniel sat by the warmth and glow of the fire, enjoying the fresh venison Daniel had roasted. After some chit-chat about what they might expect on their journey tomorrow, they decided to hit their pallets for some sleep. When Cody crawled under the shelter and stretched out on the pallet under the blankets, he was both surprised and relieved at how comfortable and warm he was. He quickly drifted off to sleep.

However, as quickly as Cody had felt sleep come over him, he seemed to wake back up. In what had been, to Cody, a blink of an eye, he had apparently experienced a night of sleep. The sky was gray with the early predawn light. Birds were singing their morning wake-up call. Off on a distant ridge, a turkey gobbled. Daniel was rekindling the fire and had a pot of coffee boiling and some venison roasting. After the two ate some breakfast, Daniel rose and poured the remaining coffee into the fire. The fire steamed and hissed in protest as he kicked at the smoldering sticks of wood to spread them apart and put them out. "We'll just leave our shelter standin', Ethan. If it's still standin' when we come back, we might just as well use it again," he said.

The two rolled up their beds and packed up the rest of camp to load back onto the pack horse. Daniel made a little extra room on the back of the animal to spread out the deer hide, or buck, as he had called it. "Gotta make sure we keep our bucks in good shape, Ethan," said Daniel. "The temperatures ought to be about right to keep 'em fresh 'till we can get back and prepare 'em proper."

The two set out on the day's journey. They had been walking along for about an hour when Daniel stopped and pointed to the northwest to a high mountain peak. "That there is Pilot Mountain," he said. "Highest point around these parts. From up there, you can see way off toward the high country. We'll take us a sashay up there and scout around for smoke. I'd like to know afore hand if we're fixin' to run into any Indians. We ain't likely to, but it's possible. There's mostly Cherokee and Catawba 'round these parts—sometimes some Shawnee or Chickasaw will wander through on huntin' trips. Those tribes don't always get along with each other, but I ain't ever had any bad run-ins with any of 'em yet. 'Course, I always make sure I have somethin' to trade with 'em—I wouldn't want to run into any with nothin' to offer."

Cody looked off to the northwest and saw the huge mountain peak. Its shape reminded Cody of a large saddle. It sloped gently from the ground at first and then nearer the top jutted up abruptly with two steep pinnacles, one smaller and lower and another very large, dome-shaped one with sheer rock cliff sides and a topping of trees.

"Indians 'round here call that mountain *Jomeokee*," said Daniel. "It means great guide, or pilot. That's why we call it Pilot Mountain. I reckon the Indians have been using it like we do, to sort of help 'em get a read on the area before they go any further."

"Are we gonna climb all the way to the top?" Cody asked.

"Well, we won't go up those rock cliffs there; they go straight up. But we'll get right up to the top of the lower point. You can see a long way from up there," Daniel answered.

Within an hour the two were ascending the mountain. After a strenuous climb, they reached the summit of the smaller of the two pinnacles. The views were spectacular, and Cody was amazed. "It sure is beautiful up here," he said.

"Yeah, you'll love the Blue Ridge, too, when we get there," Daniel replied. "The good Lord took his time when he made these mountains. He put a little somethin' extra here, you can feel it."

Cody really *could* feel it. There was something here he could sense but could not exactly define. He had noticed it on his visits to his grandpa's farm in Tennessee, too. *There is something old and wise about these mountains*, he thought.

Daniel pointed toward the western horizon, which included the blue-gray outlines of mountains that seemed much higher than the one they were currently standing on. "There it is, Ethan," he said. "The high country."

Cody had actually seen parts of those mountains before. He had been to the Smoky Mountains many times, but this was different. There was no civilization here—no tourists or tourist traps. Cody understood that as they stood there gazing westward, only a handful of white settlers had ever ventured into these parts. They and the Indians who lived here were the only human presence in these ancient mountains. He tried to comprehend this thought, but it didn't seem real to him. It was one of those imponderable notions that can boggle the mind. The two stood in silence for several minutes just staring and thinking. Of the two, Boone seemed to be looking with more of a purpose.

"I don't see any sign of Indians," he reported. "I reckon that won't hurt my feelin's none."

"Mine either," Cody replied.

Cody walked with Daniel down the mountain, and the two made their way back south to the banks of the Yadkin River. At this point, the river turned from flowing north to south to a meandering down out of the west. Although they were beginning to get into what certainly qualified as mountains to a boy from the flatlands of central Indiana, they were still about two or three days of strenuous hiking from the true high country of the Blue Ridge. Their pace was slowed by the harsher terrain and more frequent stops for the preparation of deer hides, each day following a similar pattern—rise at dawn, eat breakfast, pack gear, hike, climb high points to scan for Indian signs, hunt game, prepare hides, build shelter, eat a supper of venison, sleep, and repeat.

As they traveled farther west, Cody noticed two things about the terrain: The mountains were getting higher and steeper, and the river was getting smaller. At the end of the fourth day at the evening camp, Daniel said, "We should reach the headwaters of the Yadkin tomorrow morning, Ethan. The source of the river is just a stone's throw from the Blowing Rock. I'll take you up there. It's a special kind of place. I think you'll like it."

"I'll be lookin' forward to it," Cody answered. "So, how many hides have we got so far?"

"Let's just see," replied Daniel. "I've shot three buck deer and six does, and you've shot two does and one buck...that makes twelve bucks all together."

"Not bad for four days," said Cody.

"And we ain't really started huntin' yet," Daniel answered. "We'll hang around in this area for a week or so, and we ought to end up with twenty or thirty more, I reckon. The weather is holdin' out just right so that we ought to be able to keep these bucks in top shape if things don't change on us. Rain won't hurt 'em too much, but a warm spell would be awful hard on 'em."

The number of deer that Boone was speaking of amazed Cody. He realized that this was a time when market hunting was prevalent—that is, hunting animals for the purpose of selling their hides. In this case, he learned, the hides, or bucks, *were* money.

The next morning, after breakfast, Daniel said, "The trail turns north from here. We just have a little ways to go to reach the source of the Yadkin."

After packing up, they headed north along the now-small stream of the Yadkin. After about an hour of hiking steadily uphill, Boone stopped and pointed upward in front of them. "There is the Blowing Rock."

Cody looked up and saw a high, steep mountain with a massive outcropping of a stone cliff jutting at an angle from the summit. *It must be two thousand feet straight down from that cliff,* he thought. He noticed a stiff breeze blowing from the northeast straight down the valley they were climbing through as he continued to gaze up at the impressive natural edifice before him.

"If you liked the view from the Pilot Mountain," said Daniel, "you'll love the view from up on Blowing Rock. There's a right good story about this place, too. I'll tell it to you when we get up there."

Cody looked at up at the impressive peak, wondering how they would ever be able to get all the way up there. They began their ascent. The climb wasn't too bad at first, but it grew gradually steeper as they went. Cody could feel his thigh muscles burning under the strain of the climb. Daniel seemed to be enjoying a pleasant stroll through the park, but it was absolutely all Cody could handle to keep up. It seemed like forever to Cody before they reached the base of the rocky outcropping near the summit of the mountain. They had climbed at least 1,500 vertical feet and now had a huge rocky cliff to scale. Daniel tied the pack horse to a tree and led the way along a narrow craggy passage up the cliff. When they reached the top of the cliff, Cody felt like his breath had been taken away, not from the fatigue of the climb but from the awe-inspiring vistas from this vantage point. It was the most beautiful place Cody had ever been.

Daniel walked out to the very edge of the cliff and sat down, letting his legs hang over the side. Cody carefully followed. Cody was not exactly afraid of heights, but this was ridiculous. He peered over the edge past his dangling feet and looked straight down for nearly two thousand feet. He instantly began to feel a bit dizzy and sat back up straight.

"Gives a feller a little pause, eh?" said Daniel.

"I guess it does!" replied Cody.

As Cody looked around him over the miles and miles of endless mountain vistas, it became very clear to him how these mountains got their name. A slight haze enveloped the mountains, bathing them in a distinctly blue hue. The mountains stretched out, ridge after ridge, seemingly forever in all directions. Daniel and Cody seemed to be the only two human beings for a hundred miles, and indeed, they may have been. Cody felt tiny. He suddenly became very aware of that strange feeling again, the one he could not define. Daniel had said that God had put a little something extra in these mountains. *That must be whatever it is I feel here*, thought Cody. He didn't know how he knew it, but he could feel that this was a very ancient and sacred place. There was unheard music in the air and unspoken voices echoing up from the valleys below. The only audible sounds were of the constant wind blowing through the trees, but the sounds that Cody couldn't hear were deafening. The experience was unnerving, but by no means unpleasant.

Daniel reached into his pocket and pulled out a small swatch of deer hide. The piece of hide was about an inch square. "Watch this, Ethan," he said. He threw the piece of deer hide out over the edge of the cliff, and a moment later, Cody saw it blow straight up past them and land a few yards behind them.

"That's strange," said Cody. "Let me try that." He crawled back and retrieved the patch of hide and threw it out over the edge of the cliff. He watched in amazement as the scene repeated itself and the hide blew back up onto the cliff.

"That there leads me to the story of how this place got its name," said Daniel. "A good while back, before any white settlers ever found this place, the Catawba and the Cherokee were at war with each other. One day the daughter of a Catawba chief was up here on these rocks, and she saw a handsome Cherokee brave hunting nearby. She liked the looks of him and wanted to get his attention, so she playfully shot an arrow over in his direction. Well, she got his attention all right, and the two ended up a'fallin' in love right here on this rock. This became their rendezvous spot. One day the Cherokee warrior met the Catawba princess here and told her that his chief had called together all his warriors to attack the Catawba camp. The two Indian lovers were heartbroken. They were torn between their love for each other and their tribal allegiance. The Cherokee warrior could not face attacking his lover's people and decided to take his own life. He jumped off this very cliff. The Catawba princess was grief stricken and prayed to the Great Spirit to send her lover back to her. Just then a great wind swept up from the valley and returned the Cherokee brave

The Blowing Rock
Blowing Rock, N. C.

Silverqlo 3 R 1
BRISTOL, VA.

Blowing Rock, where Ethan Carter and Daniel Boone sat. Rain, snow, and other light objects are forced up through the walls of the gorge because of the wind's strong updraft.

to her. That wind has blown here on this cliff ever since. That's how it came to be called the Blowing Rock."

"Do you believe it?" asked Cody.

"I reckon a Cherokee brave weighs a right smart more than a little patch of deer hide, don't you?" replied Daniel. They enjoyed a good laugh and began to descend the cliff. As they neared the bottom, Cody felt the familar swimming sensation in his head and butterflies in his stomach. Before he could black out entirely, he found himself back in his bedroom at home.

PART THREE

The Journal of Landon Carter
Fort Watauga, North Carolina, 1775–76

6

Cody looked back at Ethan Carter's journal. He had thoroughly enjoyed his time in the wilderness with Daniel Boone. He had discovered in his research that within a short time, the Cherokee would be encouraged by the French to drive all the English colonists out of the frontier areas. The Yadkin Valley settlements would be attacked, and the settlers, including the Boone family, would be forced to flee northward toward the more civilized and fortified areas of Virginia colony. Cody assumed that Ethan Carter probably stayed close to the Boones through that ordeal—at least he hoped so. Cody did not relish the idea of going into the journal and living through what must have been a terrifying experience. He convinced himself that he would begin reading a new journal next time.

It was a very busy week for Cody at school. The year was winding down, and he had a lot of studying to do to prepare for the year-end final exams. In his U.S. history class, they were reviewing for a cumulative final that would cover the entire year's worth of material. That Friday afternoon, Mr. Foster, Cody's history teacher, was reviewing the French and Indian War. "Who can tell me something about the French and Indian War?" inquired Mr. Foster.

Cody's hand shot up immediately.

"Young Mr. Carter, what can you tell us?" the teacher asked.

"The French and Indian War was fought between the French and the British for control of the frontier lands in the western extremes of the American colonies. Both sides recruited the help of Indian tribes," Cody answered. "There was this one battle called the Battle of the Wilderness. It was a bad defeat for the British and Americans. George Washington was there, and so was Daniel Boone. They were lucky to survive, because the French wiped out a whole bunch of them, including their leader, General Braddock."

As Cody continued to talk, he showed no signs of slowing down. Cody's classmates had stopped any goofing off they had been doing and were suddenly looking at Cody with a bit of amazement. Mr. Foster seemed no less impressed.

Cody continued, "The French convinced the Cherokee to change their allegiance from supporting the British to supporting them. They got the Cherokee to attack the settlements on the western frontier of North Carolina and drove most of the settlers out. It was a dangerous time for American colonists to be living on the frontier fringes of the colonies. I guess that's why the French and Indian War sort of made the American colonists more unified. They felt like they needed to stick together for protection." Cody seemed to realize that he had been going on rather rapidly. He sensed that he was being watched and listened to with a lot more intensity than normal, and it started to make him self-conscious. He leaned back in his chair rather sheepishly.

"Cody, that was rather a remarkable little soliloquy," Mr. Foster said. "I don't know where you got your information, but some of the things you talked about aren't even mentioned in the textbook. I can tell you've done your research. I'm impressed!"

Cody felt proud and a little embarrassed. He hadn't realized that his little journal adventures could have a positive effect on his grade. It was a nice side benefit.

That evening, after supper, Cody decided it was time to open the next journal. He opened it to the first page and began to read.

March 1775 My name is Landon Carter. I am fifteen years old. I live in the Washington District of North Carolina in the Sycamore Shoals settlement near Fort Watauga. My father is Colonel John Carter. He is one of the commissioners for our district government, which was formed three years ago. As I write this entry, there is a tremendous gathering of Cherokee taking place along the Sycamore Shoals. A great council has been arranged by a Virginian named Richard Henderson. He is meeting with the Cherokee with intent to purchase a vast amount of land from them so that he can begin settlement of a new colony named for his company, Transylvania. . . .

As he read these words, Cody felt his head swimming in darkness and the roller-coaster sensation in his stomach returning. When he opened his eyes, he found himself on a small rise looking out over an amazing sight.

To his right was a small fort. It looked like the reproductions of historic forts he had visited. It was an irregular shape, with palisades of vertical logs that were sharpened to points on top. At random intervals along the log walls were little rooms that stuck slightly out over the edge. These, Cody assumed, were lookout rooms for guards. He could not see much inside the gate of the fort.

A large shallow stream rippled over rocks in front of Cody. On both sides, for as far up and down the shore as he could see, Indians were camped. Hundreds of plumes of campfire smoke streamed into the bluebird-spring sky.

Just off to Cody's left was a very large elm tree. Under it were gathered several men, both white and Indian. They seemed to be talking about something important. Suddenly, Cody was startled by the deep voice of a man coming from behind him.

"Quite a sight, isn't it, son?" the voice inquired.

Cody thought this man must be John Carter, if Cody was to be Landon in this journal. "How many are there?" he asked.

"Last count we had over a thousand Cherokee camped and still more on the way. It is an impressive thing to see, but it also sort of makes a man a little nervous, eh?" said John Carter.

"I never thought I would see this many in one place," said Cody. "Not too sure I ever wanted to, either."

"They've come here in peace for a council with this Henderson fellow. They are invited guests. We shouldn't have anything to fear, but I do know what you mean. Mr. Henderson and some of the chiefs are down there by the big elm. Come along if you like."

Looking again toward the elm, Cody recognized Daniel Boone, though Boone now seemed to be in his forties. The other white man, he assumed, was Richard Henderson. As he and John walked toward the tree, John began to point out the Cherokee standing in the group. Among the most notable Indians were Attakullakulla, better known to the whites by his English name, Little Carpenter, and his son, Tsi'yu-gunsini, better known as Dragging Canoe. Little Carpenter was very well known to the white settlers on the frontier as well as to the colonial government leaders. He had even been taken to Britain for a visit once. Little Carpenter was known as an easy man to negotiate with. His son, Dragging Canoe, was a different matter. Dragging Canoe was distrustful of the white settlers and saw them as a tremendous threat.

Cody could feel the hair rise up on the back of his neck and the gooseflesh beginning to crawl on his arms. He was in the presence of Indians, and powerful ones at that. He had never experienced anything close to this. He remembered being anxious about the possibility of running across Indians while hunting with Daniel Boone along the Yadkin. They had not encountered any on that trip, yet here he was in another journal, standing once again in the presence of the great Boone and real, honest-to-goodness Indians.

Cody, trying not to stare too obviously, took a good long look at Little Carpenter and Dragging Canoe. They cut impressive figures. Little Carpenter appeared to be in his forties. Across his chest, he wore a beaded garment with multicolored chevron patterns. Around his waist hung a deerskin loincloth that reached to just above his knees, and he wore nearly knee-high deer-hide boots. A single eagle feather hung down from the jet-black hair that covered part of his face. His skin was a deep brownish-almond color. Distinguished-looking lines and wrinkles were beginning to form around the corners of his eyes and mouth. He was a short man—Cody estimated him to be just over five feet tall—but the overall impression he made was more than impressive enough to cover any height deficiency.

Dragging Canoe was just as impressive, but for other reasons. He was dressed almost identically to his father. His skin was almost the same hue, but he had a pock-marked face. Cody wondered if the scars were due to smallpox, which he knew often left such marks on survivors of the illness. Dragging Canoe was also much taller than his father, having attained a height of some-where over five-and-a-half feet, Cody guessed. Something else distinguished Dragging Canoe from his father—his countenance. Anyone who looked

The image on this postcard depicts the treaty council at Sycamore Shoals in which Richard Henderson and Daniel Boone met with the Cherokee, including Little Carpenter and Drag-ging Canoe, to purchase lands in Kentucky and Tennessee for the Transylvania Colony. ("West lunette, the treaty of Wataga: the Cherokee Indians selling Kentucky to the Transyl-vania Land Company," Newton Owen Postcard Collection, University of Louisville Archives and Records Center, Louisville, Kentucky)

Dragging Canoe in the face could see he was a man who meant business. He didn't strike Cody as a person one would want to have as an enemy.

John finally introduced Cody to the men in the group. "Landon, these are our guests, Little Carpenter and Dragging Canoe. Gentlemen, this is my son, Landon." The two Indians bowed slightly, and Cody followed suit. "And this is Richard Henderson of the Transylvania Land Company. He is here to put the finishing touches on a large purchase of land from the Cherokee. That is why all these people are gathered. It will be an historic occasion, to be sure." Henderson extended his hand, and Cody gave his best firm handshake. "And this gentleman is Daniel Boone," said John, nodding to a man who was all too familiar to Cody.

"Pleased to make yer acquaintance, Landon," said Boone as he reached out to shake Cody's hand. Boone still looked very much the same as he had when Cody had met him in 1755. He was dressed in his buckskins and wide-brimmed, beaver-fur hat. The only changes were a few more wrinkles on his face and a slightly more filled-out frame. He still looked the very picture of a pioneer mountain man. Cody wanted to ask Boone whatever became of Ethan Carter, but the words would not come.

Later that afternoon, the official treaty council began. Cody positioned himself in a good spot to view the ceremony. Henderson laid out his proposal for the purchase of all the lands lying between the Cumberland River and Cumberland Mountains to the south, the Kentucky River to the east, and the Ohio River to the north and west. In exchange for this land (amounting to more than twenty million acres), Henderson would pay the Cherokee two thousand pounds sterling and goods worth a total of about eight thousand additional pounds.

In turn, the different Cherokee chiefs were permitted some time to get up and speak their minds about the treaty. Most of the chiefs were in favor of making the deal, including Little Carpenter. One of the notable exceptions was Dragging Canoe, who was quite agitated.

Cody looked on nervously when it was Dragging Canoe's turn to speak. Anyone who had been watching him during the proceedings knew that what he was about to say would not be any kind of endorsement for this purchase. Dragging Canoe walked intently to the speaking area and glared out at the crowd. Cody sensed himself preparing to record every word in his mind. Dragging Canoe began to speak.

Whole Indian nations have melted away like snowballs in the sun before the white man's advance. They leave scarcely a name of our people. . . . Where are the Delawares? They have been reduced to a mere shadow of their former greatness. We had hoped that the white men would not be willing to travel beyond the mountains. Now that hope is gone. They have passed the mountains, and have settled upon Cherokee land. They wish to have that action sanctioned by treaty. When that is gained, the same encroaching spirit will lead them upon other land of the Cherokees. The Cherokees will be asked again to give up land. Finally the whole country, which the Cherokees and their fathers have so long occupied, will be demanded, and the remains of Ani-Yunwiya, THE REAL PEOPLE, once so great and formidable, will be compelled to seek refuge in some distant wilderness. There they will be permitted to stay only a short while, until they again see the advancing flags of the same greedy men. . . . The extinction of the whole race will be proclaimed. Should we not therefore run all risks, and endure all consequences, rather than submit to further loss of our country? Such treaties may be alright for men who are too old to hunt or fight. As for me, I have my young warriors around me. We will have our lands. A-WANINSKI, I have spoken.

If the hairs had not been standing up on the back of Cody's neck before, they surely were now. Dragging Canoe's chilling and prophetic speech resonated all around the assembled crowd. In the end, however, it did nothing to prevent the inevitable deal from taking place. The Treaty of Sycamore Shoals was signed, and Henderson had his land. All that was left for him to do now was to open it up for settlement and to form his new colony called Transylvania.

As Cody stood there taking in this historic scene, he was once again startled by John Carter. "Well, I guess that is that. We'll see if this holds up, but between you and me, son, I have my doubts."

"What kind of doubts? What do you mean?" Cody asked.

"Doubts about whether this whole transaction is even legal," answered John. "A lot of folks are whispering that Henderson is trying to rush this deal through and doesn't really have the power to do it. Some of the Cherokee are even snickering about this deal, saying they don't even claim ownership of the land they sold. They don't live in those lands, no Indians do, for the most part. It goes against their beliefs to live in that land. It is sacred land to them—land that they set apart only to hunt in. That land is shared by these Cherokee and

Wataugah Purchase

This Indenture made this nineteenth day of March in the year of our Lord Christ one thousand seven hundred and seventy five Between Oconistoto chief Warrier and first representative of the Cherokee Nation or tribe of Indians & Atacullaculla & Savan-nucah otherwise Coronoh for themselves and the rest of the whole nation being the Aborigines and sole owners by occupancy from the beginning of time of the Lands on the waters of Holston & Wataugah rivers & other Lands & Territories thereunto belonging of the one part and Charles Robertson of the Settlement of Wataugah of the other part Witnesseth, that the said Oconistoto for himself and the rest of the said Nation of Indians for and in consideration of [...] thousand pounds of Lawful money of Great Brittain to them in hand paid by the said Charles Robertson the receipt whereof the said Oconistoto and the whole nation do and for themselves and their whole Tribe of people have granted bargained and sold aliened enfeoff'd released and confirmed and by these presents do grant bargain sell alien enfeoff release and confirm unto him the said Charles Robertson his heirs and assigns for ever all that tract territory or parcel of Land on the waters of Wataugah Holston and great Canaway or New River Beginning on the on the south or south west side of Holston River six English Miles above the long Island in said river thence a direct line [...] a So. W. course to the ridge which divides the waters of Watau-gah from the waters of Nonachuckeh thence along the various courses of said ridge nearly a south east course to the blue ridge or line dividing North Carolina from the Cherokee Lands thence along the various courses of said ridge to the Virginia line thence West along the Virginia line to Holston [...]

In the Watauga Purchase, signed at the treaty council at Sycamore Shoals, the Cherokee Nation agreed to sell territory on the Watauga and Holston Rivers in what is now northeastern Tennessee.

the Shawnee, who come down from the north to hunt there. There is a very good chance that this deal will not be allowed to happen by the governments of North Carolina, Virginia, or Britain. It all seems a little shady to me. But then again, we here in the Watauga Settlements are standing on shaky legal footing as it is. We really aren't supposed to be here, according to the King's Proclamation of 1763."

Cody hadn't been familiar with the story of the Treaty of Sycamore Shoals or the Transylvania Colony, but he knew all about the Proclamation of 1763. He remembered that it was a law placed on the colonies by King George III that made settlement west of the Appalachian Mountains illegal. As he recalled, this law was not popular with the American colonists. In fact, it was one of the first major wedges that separated the colonies and their mother country. Now Cody could see what Carter was saying. Everyone living west of the Appalachians in 1775 was technically breaking the law. That, coupled with some other aspects of the law that addressed who could make treaties with Indians and who actually had the rightful claim to the land being purchased made Henderson's treaty a questionable one at best.

"Still," continued Carter, "I don't see a man like Richard Henderson letting anything stand in his way. I look for him to push right on with his plans to start this new colony whether it's legal or not. He has already hired Daniel Boone to open up the trail for settlement. Boone is going to be leaving from here and will start widening the trail through the Cumberland Gap. He is already gathering the first group of investors to go with him. I hear he has around thirty lined up to go right away. I don't see how this can possibly work out, but with a man like Richard Henderson in charge, well, it just might not be wise to bet against him."

As Cody considered John's words, he began to feel a swimming sensation in his head. Just as everything began to go dark, he found himself back in his bedroom.

7

Cody sat at his desk staring down at the words of Landon Carter. He was still trying to comprehend the fact that he had just been in the presence of more than a thousand Cherokee. Cody sensed the image would be burned into his brain as long as he lived. He realized that no living person had ever gotten to be an eyewitness to what he had just seen—a treaty council. He was once again learning things he had never known from his history classes. He had never heard of a colony called Transylvania. The only Transylvania Cody ever remembered hearing about was where Dracula came from, and he was pretty sure that wasn't near Kentucky!

Cody glanced at the alarm clock next to his bed and saw that it was still early in the evening. He felt like going right back to his reading, but he heard his father in the living room downstairs. One question had puzzled Cody ever since his grandfather had returned to Tennessee: Why had Grandpa brought the journals to him and not his father? Hadn't his father kept a journal? If not, why? Cody finally decided he would ask his dad about this, so he went downstairs.

"Hey, Dad," said Cody. "Do you have a second?" Many times Cody's dad didn't have a second. As a pharmaceutical sales representative for the Eli Lilly Company, Mark Carter provided a good living for his family but was often on the road for days on end. He was a good and caring father but was not always around when Cody wanted him to be. For this reason, sometimes Cody found it awkward to approach his dad with serious questions, so he usually saved those for his mother.

"Sure, Cody. What's on your mind?" replied Cody's father.

"It's just a question I have been meaning to ask you about my journals," said Cody. "You know, the ones Grandpa brought me to read." As he mentioned the journals, Cody sensed his father stiffen a bit.

"What about them, son?" his father replied.

"Well, it's what Grandpa said about the Carter family tradition," Cody answered. "He said that Carters started journaling in their teens and then got to read the stories of all the Carter teens before them. I was just wondering why it is that with you and me, the tradition seemed to skip a generation. Didn't you want to take part in the tradition, Dad?"

Cody's father paused for so long before speaking that Cody grew uncomfortable. "I was wondering if you were going to ask me about this," his father said carefully. "Actually, I did start to do the journaling thing. My dad gave me a box of journals when I was about your age, and I started reading like you—but I couldn't take it."

Cody felt a chill run up his spine. His father must have had some similar experiences of being transported into the lives of their ancestors when he read the journals.

His father continued. "Cody, when you read those journals, does any-thing—*funny*—happen to you?"

There it is, Cody thought. His suspicions had been correct. He was relieved to learn that he was not the only person who had experienced such strange happenings while reading the journals, but also felt curious as to why his dad seemed to feel so negatively about his own experiences.

"Yes," replied Cody. "It happens every time. I start to read and the next thing I know, I am *living* the words. I am inside the body of the person who wrote the journal. It is so freaky. Is that what happened to you too, Dad?"

"Well, it certainly sounds like it," his father replied, "but I only opened one journal and only read one time." He paused. He seemed to be measuring his words again, and perhaps censoring some of them. "Do you enjoy reading the journals?"

"Yes, I think it's awesome!" Cody replied excitedly. "I have been scared a few times, but you wouldn't believe what I have experienced. I got to kill a deer—an eight-point buck! I got to meet Daniel Boone—the *real* Daniel Boone—he was my friend! We went on a hunting trip through the Blue Ridge Mountains. I even met him again twenty-some years later—and we were in a crowd of about a thousand Cherokee!"

His father cut him short, bringing Cody's mood down a few notches. "In-dians? Son, I am not trying to scare you or discourage you, but I just have to warn you—you might want to think about what you could be getting into. I'm not trying to tell you that you are in any sort of physical danger; lots of Carters have read every word of those journals and have come out ok. Your grandpa is one of them. I am just saying that they may not be for everyone—emotionally speaking."

"Are you trying to say why you didn't read any more than you did, Dad?" Cody asked.

"You mentioned seeing Indians," his father replied. "Have you had any encounters that seemed dangerous?"

"Well," Cody answered, "I was pretty nervous being in a big crowd of Indians, but I don't think I would call it dangerous. Why do you ask?" His father's cryptic question had increased Cody's nervousness.

"When I went into the journal that one time," his father said, "I was around Indians, too. I can't even remember the name of the journal, it has been so long ago, but it was in the Indiana Territory. I have forgotten some of the details, but I will just tell you that I had some experiences with Indians that I have tried to forget ever since. I came out okay, but I am telling you to be careful in making your decisions. Maybe you could experience what I did and be fine with it, but I wouldn't do it again—in fact, I stopped right there and never went back."

Cody could sense that his dad was not telling him any details for a reason. He wasn't sure why, but he knew he shouldn't press for more information. "I have had some emotional experiences, but nothing too bad, yet," he said.

"I am not trying to scare you, just prepare you," stated his father. "There might be some things that are tough to go through in those journals. I am not trying to tell you what to do or what not to do. That is up to you. Just know that it might not all be pleasant."

Cody already had experienced enough in the journals to have some understanding of what his father was trying to tell him. He had been through some emotional highs and lows. But he wondered what had so rattled his dad. It was just one more thing to think about as he continued on his very strange journey through the Carter journals.

Cody said goodnight to his dad and headed back to his room. He decided to read some more of the Landon Carter journal before turning in for the night. Sitting down with the journal, he turned the page and began to read.

July, 1776 Exciting but troubled times—Word has reached us of a Declaration of Independence being issued by the Continental Congress in Philadelphia. Apparently, the trouble with Britain has reached a point of no return. The war that started in Massachusetts last year is apparently not to be avoided. We have declared ourselves to be an independent nation—the United States of America. Most of us here in the Washington District consider ourselves

Independence Hall in Philadelphia as it appeared in 1776. The Declaration of Independence was adopted here on July 4, 1776.

staunch patriots, though many of us have acquaintances and loved ones whose loyalties remain with the Crown. Though we have remained far from the battles between the British and American armies, we are no less concerned. Our trouble is expected to come in the form of Indians. . . .

As Cody read these words, he began to feel himself being pulled back into the journal. This time he found himself within the walls of Fort Watauga in one of several small cabins along the interior of the palisade wall. Inside the cabin were John Carter and several other men that Cody did not recognize, one of whom was evidently in the middle of delivering some sobering news, based on the men's grim expressions. John must have noticed Cody's confusion. He leaned over and, nodding toward the man who was speaking, whispered, "John Sevier has just returned from settlements along the Nolichucky River, where the new fort is under construction. The Cherokee woman Nanye-hi, also called Nancy Ward, came to warn the settlers that her cousin Dragging Canoe was going to lead an attack. The British have supplied him with guns and ammunition. Nanye-hi is a Beloved Woman, a peacemaker in tribal councils, and unlike her cousin, she believes the whites and Indians can coexist peaceably."

"The settlements of the Nolichucky are preparing to evacuate," Sevier was now saying. "The fort is not nearly finished enough to be a safe haven. Most of the Fort Lee settlers will be headed up here to join us at Fort Watauga. Eaton's Station is bracing for trouble, too. They are a little better fortified than Fort Lee. Hopefully, they will be able to fight off any attacks. Be prepared to make some room. Things could get a little crowded around this place, and soon."

Some days seemed to pass as scores of settlers fleeing from the Fort Lee area came to the Watauga to join forces. The little fort was soon home to more than 150 settlers along with a garrison of some seventy-five militia. As the Commissioner of Safety for the Watauga settlements, John Carter was in charge of the militia.

As predicted, a war party, led by Dragging Canoe, soon began to launch attacks on the settlements, beginning with Fort Lee. Fort Lee and the surrounding farms were abandoned when the attacks began. The Indians burned down the unfinished fort and destroyed many of the farms. They had begun to work their way toward Eaton's Station when word reached Fort Watauga of their movements.

At Fort Watauga, settlers tried to make the best of the cramped conditions. Many cows, goats, and pigs brought along with the Fort Lee settlers joined the herds of the Wataugans, grazing outside the walls of the fort. Part of the daily regimen of the settlers, particularly the women, was to venture out and gather in their cattle twice a day for milking. Armed sentries were always posted in the watchtowers before anyone went outside the fort.

Early one morning, Cody was milling around talking with some of the newcomers from Fort Lee when he heard a clattering outside the gates. Two armed riders dismounted from their exhausted horses and were let inside. The men had come at full gallop from the direction of Eaton's Station. They were obviously dirty, disheveled, and very worked up. They were wearing the mismatched garb of local militia. As their horses were led away to the watering trough near the center of the fort's courtyard, one of the men stepped forward and asked to talk to John Carter.

"That's my father. I will go and get him," Cody said.

Cody sprinted toward the little cabin where the Carters lived inside the fort. He ran inside and said, "Father, there are some men outside to see you. They came from Eaton's Station—they say it's urgent."

"Send them in," said John.

Cody quickly returned with the two spent-looking soldiers, and John motioned for them and his son to join him around the table.

"What is all this about?" asked John.

John Sevier (1745–1815) was a leader of the Sycamore Shoals settlements and participated in the Battle of Kings Mountain. He became the governor of the state of Franklin and later the first governor of Tennessee.

"Sir, I'm Corporal Donner and this here is Private Logan," said the soldier, nodding to his companion. "We come to tell you there has been an attempted attack on Eaton's Station by Dragging Canoe and some of his warriors. We were plumb lucky to find out they were comin' before they got all the way to us. We were able to get us up a platoon and went out to meet 'em before they could get to the settlements. We opened up on 'em and had a right smart battle. By our count we killed thirteen of them savages—at least that's how many scalps we collected—and we wounded more than that. Logan here put a bullet in ol' Dragging Canoe himself. Didn't hit him good enough to kill 'im though, but he'll know he's been in a scrap, that's fer sure!"

Cody was slightly stunned by what he had just heard. Did Donner really just say that they had collected the scalps of the dead Indians? He knew that various Indian tribes practiced the grisly art of scalping their victims. It was a sort of trophy to them—proof of their kills. He remembered hearing Edward Carter Sr.'s gut-wrenching account of having nearly witnessed the scalping of his father during the Tuscarora Wars. Cody had always been under the impression that Indians scalped whites, not the other way around, but apparently, this practice must have gone both ways.

"Where are the Indians now?" asked John.

"We ran 'em off, but they'll be back. I look fer 'em to head this way next. I'm sure ol' Dragging Canoe will organize more of his men, and he'll probably get help from some other chiefs around here. We were sent here to warn you to be lookin' fer 'em."

"Thank you, gentlemen," replied John. "We most certainly will keep a sharp eye out. You two look like you could use a hot meal and a good night's rest. I am sure your horses could use the rest, as well. Why don't you join us here tonight, and you can go back tomorrow and take a better survey on any damage done. We don't have much in the way of extra room, but we will be glad to spare you any we can."

As John stood to begin arrangements to shelter the two men, Cody felt himself being pulled out of the journal. When he opened his eyes, he found himself back in his bedroom.

8

Cody looked at the clock on his nightstand and was surprised to see it read eleven o'clock. He didn't feel the least bit tired. He had too many thoughts racing through his head to sleep. He thought back upon what his dad had said earlier. His dad may not have been the Daniel Boone type, but Cody had never known him to be wimpy in any way. Whatever he had experienced in his one trip into the journals must have shaken him up pretty badly. All Cody really knew was that his dad's experience had taken place in the Indiana Territory and that it involved Indians. Cody was beginning to think that Landon Carter was about to have a run-in with Indians, but not in the Indiana Territory. As he sat and mulled over his options, Cody finally decided that he had come too far to turn back now. He was going to see this thing through, or try his best to, at least. He decided to take one more look at the Landon Carter journal before trying to sleep. He found his place and began to read.

> *July 21, 1776 Our worst fears were realized this morning—and we were somehow caught off guard. Several women were outside the fort walls doing their morning milking when a scream was heard. . . .*

As he read these words, Cody felt himself immediately transported back to Fort Watauga. His arrival found him sprinting full speed across the fort's courtyard in a near panic. He heard a woman's piercing scream coming from outside the fort walls. He bounded up a ladder that led to a platform walkway below the top of the palisade wall. As he looked out over the pointed ends of the logs, he saw several women clutching their long dresses and running as fast as they could go toward the fort's gates. He looked down to the gates and saw several of the men gathering there. When he glanced back over the wall, he saw why the women were running. About a dozen Cherokee warriors were sprinting toward them from the nearby woods.

A contemporary photograph of the reconstruction of Fort Watauga, located in Tennessee's Sycamore Shoals State Historic Park.

The warriors were a terrifying sight to behold. They were nearly naked, except for loincloths and breastplates that appeared to be made of bones. Their faces and arms were covered in red and black paint. Some were carrying rifles, while others appeared only to be wielding tomahawks or bows and arrows. The most frightening aspect of the approaching Indians was the earsplitting noises they were emitting. Their war whoops sounded like the yipping of a frenzied pack of coyotes hot on the heels of a fawn. The sound made Cody feel sick to his stomach. He knew at once he would never forget it.

Suddenly, the sick feeling in Cody's gut intensified as he realized what the men at the gates were preparing to do—they were about to shut them! All the settlers inside the fort were yelling at the women caught outside to run faster. The gates had to be closed to protect all those inside. The women had to make it in before the gates were shut, and from the looks of things, it was going to be close. Cody watched with relief as the first four women made it through the gate, but his relief quickly turned to horror as he realized that one of the women was clearly not going to make it into the safety of the fort.

"One of them's still out there!" Cody shouted. "She's going to be locked out!"

By this time, the guards had opened fire on the approaching Indians and forced them to drop down. The Indians, in turn, began firing back toward the fort. They were still just out of accurate rifle range, but at least it provided the woman with some cover and bought her some time.

Then John Sevier came running up a ladder about fifty feet to Cody's left. Sevier looked out over the wall and shouted to the stranded woman, "This way, Bonnie Kate! Come grab my hand!"

Sevier positioned himself between two of the sharpened points atop the palisade and leaned down as far as he could so that his hand hung down toward the ground. Cody watched as the terrified woman stumbled over and reached up for Sevier's hand. He was able to get a good purchase on her.

"Hold on tight, Bonnie Kate," said Sevier. "I'm going to pull you up. Use your feet against the wall for leverage."

Bonnie Kate did as she was told and sort of walked her way up the wall with her feet as Sevier pulled her up by the arms. When she got near the top, Sevier was able to get a better grip, and he gave one more mighty heave to pull her to safety. Once inside, she collapsed in Sevier's arms and buried her face in his shoulder, sobbing uncontrollably. The crowd that had gathered below Sevier gave a mighty *huzzah*! When she had calmed down, Bonnie Kate rejoined the other women who had been ambushed. Sevier returned to stand guard with some of the militia.

The Cherokee raid then turned into a siege. The fort was a fairly safe refuge for those inside, as long as they stayed inside. The Indians had it surrounded but seemed content for the next few hours to sit tight and watch from a safe distance. Occasional volleys of gunfire were exchanged, but no bullets seemed to find a mark. John Carter and Sevier called a meeting in the main cabin with some of the leading men to hatch a plan for what to do next. Cody was there with them.

John spoke up first. "Well, gentlemen, we can certainly count ourselves fortunate that we didn't lose any souls in that attack—but it was a little too close for comfort. Thanks to Mr. Sevier's quick action, we were able to get all of our women safely back inside the fort. We have a lot of livestock out there, though. I am sure the Indians will kill or steal whatever they can of our cattle."

Sevier added, "We have enough provisions to last us for a while, but if the Indians maintain this siege over a prolonged period, we might have to plan to send some people out under armed guard to bring in water or food."

The assembled men continued to make contingency plans for all possible scenarios. It was mentioned at one point that large kettles of water should be kept boiling in the courtyard. Cody assumed that was for potential medical emergencies, but he didn't know for sure.

John Sevier helping his future wife, Bonnie Kate Sherrill, over the fort wall during the siege of Fort Watauga, July 20, 1776.

The next morning, Cody was taking a turn in a watchtower. He was looking out over the open field in the general direction from which the Indians had come screaming out of the woods. He felt goosebumps rise up on his arms and neck as he recalled the horrifying coyote-like war yips that had come out of the painted warriors the day before. Suddenly, Cody thought he caught a glimpse of movement coming from his right. He spun around and noticed four Indians with torches attempting to sneak up to the wall of the fort just around a corner from his position. The Indians obviously had been studying the layout of the fort well because they had chosen to approach the part of the wall that was most vulnerable to attack. It was the place that was most difficult to cover with gunfire. They were closing in. Cody realized that they intended to try to set fire to the fort.

"Indians approaching from the north!" Cody called out. "I can't shoot at them from here."

Then Cody began to understand the purpose of the boiling water. He watched as several men raced out to the kettle and formed a bucket brigade. The men formed a line that led from the kettle to a ladder on the wall that was under attack. They began passing buckets of the scalding hot liquid quickly down the line and up the ladder. When several buckets had been gathered at the top, the men crouched there and waited patiently until the Indians had gotten just to the base of the wall. Then, in one motion, the group stood and poured the contents of their buckets down upon the unsuspecting band of warriors. The boiling water rained down upon the Indians, who howled in terrible pain, dropped their torches, and ran back in the direction from which they had come. The bucket bearers erupted in victorious laughter and celebration, slapping each other on the back with delight. Cody smiled at the cleverness of this devilish little defensive strategy.

Later that day, after an afternoon free of any Indian sightings, some in the fort were convinced the siege was over. It was decided that the gates would be opened slightly and that any men who wished to risk a venture outside could do so at their own peril. Some of the men wanted to go and check on the status of their livestock. One of them was a young man named Tom Moore. He went out to track down a missing cow and ventured out near the wood line. One of the guards heard him scream out, but it was too late. Moore was captured by the Indians. As the other settlers retreated behind the safety of the fort's closed gates, Cody felt himself being transported back to his bedroom.

PART FOUR

The Journal of Annabelle Carter
State of Franklin, 1788

9

Cody awoke late. He had put in a pretty long night. After experiencing the Indian siege on Fort Watauga, he had gone back one more time to finish up the last of Landon Carter's journal. He learned that the siege of the fort had ended later that same summer, when Virginia sent militia to reinforce the fortifications. He then had heard John Sevier tell the story of the Battle of Kings Mountain, which had taken place in the fall of 1780. Landon Carter was a grown man of twenty by that time, but still had taken the time to enter the story in his journal. Sevier and a man named Isaac Shelby had recruited hundreds of volunteer soldiers at Sycamore Shoals in response to a report that the British were intent on sending troops over the Blue Ridge to flush out any settlements west of the mountains. A British major named Patrick Ferguson was storming through the Carolinas with the intention of carrying out that plan. Sevier had other plans, however. He and Shelby mustered their make-shift army and went on the offensive.

They left from Sycamore Shoals on September 25 and marched to the southwest over the mountains to engage Ferguson's army. By October 7, Sevier's men had reached the British and surprised them as they camped on a small hill in South Carolina that had been named Kings Mountain by the British. Using Indian tactics and guerilla warfare, Sevier's "Overmountain Men," as they came to be called, dominated Ferguson's army. Ferguson and more than 150 of his troops were killed.

Cody had then turned to the Internet to learn more about the battle. It had been very costly to the British plan of overtaking the Carolinas. Other key American victories in the area, including the Battle of Cowpens one day earlier and just a short distance away, led British General Lord Charles Cornwallis to abandon his plans in the Carolinas. Sevier had become a well-known hero as a result of these efforts.

With the completion of Landon's journal, Cody decided to take a break, so he spent that Saturday with some of his friends playing football at the park.

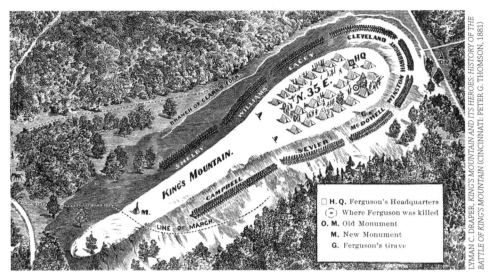

LYMAN C. DRAPER, *KING'S MOUNTAIN AND ITS HEROES: HISTORY OF THE BATTLE OF KING'S MOUNTAIN* (CINCINNATI: PETER G. THOMSON, 1881)

This diagram of the Battle of Kings Mountain depicts the Overmountain Men surrounding British Major Patrick Ferguson's encampment on Kings Mountain.

He had wanted to tell them about what he was experiencing with the journals, but had decided they would probably not believe him and would laugh at him. It felt lonely to have all these experiences and not be able to tell anyone. Cody had thought about sharing his stories with his dad again, but given the negative experience his father had with the journals, that option was questionable. Cody decided he would just ride this out alone for now. Maybe he would talk to his grandpa about it later.

After supper, Cody went to his room and selected the next journal in the time line. He opened the cover and began to read.

> *March 1788 My name is Annabelle Carter. Most folks call me Anne or Annie. I am sixteen years old. I live in Greeneville, capital of the State of Franklin, with my parents, Nancy and David Carter. Times have been hard here for the last several years . . . from the very beginning really. My uncle is Landon Carter. He is the Speaker of the Senate for the State of Franklin. He knows Governor John Sevier well. I am privy to a lot of information about the status of our young, struggling government. I fear we won't be able to hold out much longer. . . .*

What in the world is the State of Franklin? Cody thought. *And Annabelle?* Was he really going to have to be a girl this time? So far he hadn't felt anything strange happening, and he found that to be a great relief. He decided to read on.

Of late, our settlements have been under nearly constant harassment by Indians. The Cherokee, Chickamauga, and Chickasaw have been attacking farms throughout the area. . . .

As he read these words, Cody felt his head swimming and the roller-coaster butterflies returning. Like it or not, he was being transported into the journal. When he opened his eyes, he found himself sitting at a writing table. As he glanced down at himself, he noticed he was wearing a dress. *You have got to be kidding me*, Cody thought.

Before he had a chance to examine his situation any further, Cody sensed someone walking into the room. "Back at your journal, I see," said the woman who entered the room. "Working on your history of the state of Franklin?"

"Y-yes," Cody responded uncertainly.

"Well, Annie dear, you might be just the perfect person to record such a history," answered the woman. Cody realized she must be Annabelle's mother, Nancy Carter. "You are a keen observer, and you also have your Uncle Landon who knows as much about the workings of this government as anyone. He has been involved in it since the beginning—before the beginning actually. He will be coming for supper tonight. I am sure he will be delighted to hear that you are planning to do this."

Cody wondered if this Uncle Landon was the same Landon whose journal he had just finished. He wasn't sure because he had no idea where he was, having never heard of the state of Franklin. Cody noticed right away that these people seemed to be better educated than some of the others in journals he had visited. He also noticed that this house was no cabin. It had wood-frame construction, and the room he was in contained fine furniture, a hardwood floor, a stone hearth fireplace, and all the other adornments that accompany the homes of the well-to-do. It reminded Cody of historic homes of famous people he had visited on family vacations.

"Come now and help me prepare tonight's supper," said Nancy.

Cody followed the woman toward the kitchen. Along the way, they passed a large oval mirror on a wooden stand. Cody stole a quick glance at his reflection. He saw a very lovely teenage girl with curly blonde locks flowing out from under a blue cap. The dress she was wearing was the same pale blue as the cap and had long sleeves with white lace around the cuffs and the neckline. The hemline reached almost to the floor.

When they reached the kitchen, Cody was surprised to see a middle-aged, rather plump black woman standing at the stove. "Chicken's 'bout done, Miss Nancy," said the woman.

"Thanks, Bessie dear," replied Nancy. "Annie and I will prepare a salad, and you can set the table. Oh, and set an extra place for Master David's brother Landon. He'll be joining us this evening."

"Yes'm," replied Bessie.

A man arrived at the house a few minutes later and made small talk with Nancy about his day at his law office. In town, he had heard several settlers from surrounding farms complaining that it was becoming impossible for them to live there due to the constant threat from Indian attacks. "It's getting worse, Nancy," said the man. "I am afraid we're going to have to get on bended knee soon and beg North Carolina to take us back. We just don't have the resources to go it alone."

Cody assumed the man was Annabelle's father, David. He listened to the conversation with interest. He still was unsure what was going on here, but he had a few more pieces of the puzzle. He knew he was in a place called the state of Franklin. Though he had never heard of this place, from what David had just said, it must have been a part of North Carolina that had somehow become independent. Cody had never even heard of such a thing. It certainly wasn't in his history book.

After the food was prepared and the table set, he was told to go prepare for supper. As he entered Annabelle's bedroom, Cody looked around and found it to be very nice. He noticed that there was a much more normal-looking bed than the ones he had experienced in the previous journals. There was a vanity table with a small padded bench in front of it and a tilting, rectangular mirror mounted at the back of the table. Cody once again found himself staring into the reflection of a lovely teenage girl; he would never even be able to work up the nerve to speak to her back home. Cody picked up a hairbrush from the table and brushed his long hair. A powder puff and small porcelain vial with a cork stopper also lay on the table, but because Cody wasn't sure what Annie would have done with them, he decided it was safer to just make sure his face was clean and the rest of him was at least presentable.

Cody heard some muffled voices outside the bedroom door. It sounded like Uncle Landon must have arrived. He left the room and saw a man standing near the entryway, hat and walking stick in hand. He had just finished greeting David and Nancy, and now he turned his attention toward Cody. "Annie, come here and give us a hug," said Landon. Cody knew it would seem strange if Annie refused, so he did as Landon requested.

The John and Landon Carter mansion in Elizabethton, Tennessee, ca. 1950. Built around 1780, the mansion is the only remaining artifact of the Watauga Association, which predated the state of Franklin. Many Watauga Association members and their families became citizens of the state of Franklin.

Landon Carter was an impressive-looking man. He was dressed in a formal suit and looked like someone important, just like the pictures of old-time presidents or senators that Cody had seen in textbooks. "Your parents tell me you would like to write the history of Franklin," said Landon. "I think that is great news. If you need any information from me, I will be most happy to help you."

"Thanks," answered Cody. "I will probably need to take full advantage of that."

"First, I'd like to sit down to some of that delicious chicken I am smelling," smiled Landon.

As the family sat down around the table and Bessie began serving up the meal, Cody's head was whirling. This was a part of American history that he had no prior knowledge of. Had there really been a whole state that was left out of the history books? Why had he never heard of this? Dresses or no dresses, girl or no girl, Cody just had to find out more about this state of Franklin.

After supper, Cody sat down in the parlor with Uncle Landon and prepared to make some notes on their conversation. He wanted to know the story of Franklin from the beginning.

"Tell me a little bit about why Franklin split away from North Carolina, if you don't mind," Cody requested.

"Sure," Landon answered. "I suppose you were a little too young to be following politics then, weren't you? You know how the Watauga settlements and the other white settlements out here, west of the mountains, are so isolated? You know how it sometimes feels like we are left to fend for ourselves? People here have built up a little resentment during the years when North Carolina never seemed to deem us important enough to offer much support. Well, once the war with Britain was won, and the United States was able to back up our claim of independence, the federal government was in terrible debt. In 1784 North Carolina offered to give the Congress of Confederation all its land between the Alleghenies and the Mississippi River. Now, that sounds like a mighty generous thing to do, but once again, we settlers out here felt like we were being completely overlooked. Our state just turned its back on us and gave us away! It didn't sit well with us—not one bit. We had worked hard to try to establish ourselves here. We opened this area up and improved it. We had no idea what the federal government planned to do with this land. For all we knew, they might have sold it to Spain or France to make some fast money."

"Well, after a few months, word reached us that North Carolina had withdrawn their offer to give our land to the federal government. Maybe we should have let well enough alone when we learned that, but by that time, we had gotten ourselves all worked up with our own spirit of independence. We certainly didn't feel like we could trust North Carolina to have our best interests anymore. So, on August 23, 1784, settlements from Washington, Sullivan, and Greene Counties sent delegates to Jonesborough. We met to discuss our options, and it was decided that we would declare our independence from North Carolina. It took us a few months to hammer out a constitution and government. By the spring of 1785, we felt ready to apply for statehood. We called our state *Frankland* at that time. On May 16, delegates from Frankland delivered a petition to the Continental Congress for admission to the United States of America. We got a majority—seven of the states voted to accept us, but under the Articles of Confederation, approval required a two-thirds majority, so we came up a little short. Someone got the idea to rename our state in honor of Benjamin Franklin in order to sort of butter him up to get him to use his influence to sway a few more votes. We changed the name to Franklin, but Mr. Franklin politely declined to offer us his help. So we have been an entity all our own ever since—a country unto ourselves. As you know, that has not been easy."

As Landon finished his explanation, Cody felt the familiar swimming sensation in his head and things began to go dark. Suddenly, he found himself back in his bedroom.

10

Cody glanced at his alarm clock and saw it was early afternoon. He felt a little annoyed and unnerved after just experiencing a journal trip in the person of a girl, but he was learning some information he had never known. He looked out his window and saw that it was raining steadily, washing away any plans for outdoor fun. Disappointed, he headed downstairs and popped a couple of waffles in the toaster and poured a glass of milk. As he watched TV and ate his snack, he decided he might as well read a little more from Annie's journal. It was strange being a girl, but he mustered the courage to dive back in and hope for the best.

After returning to his room, Cody found the spot in the journal where he had last been and began to read.

Just as Uncle Landon had finished relating the history of the beginning of the government of Franklin, we were interrupted by a horse and rider outside the house. It was George Finchum and he was distraught. . . .

Again Cody's insides were full of butterflies. When he opened his eyes this time, he found himself standing by the front door of the Carter home. Uncle Landon was with Nancy and David, and they had all rushed to the door to see about the commotion outside. A squat, portly, middle-aged man was dismounting from his horse and seemed agitated. "Evenin' folks. Sorry to bother you, but I have the watch tonight and I am right sure there are Cherokee afoot nearby. I seen one a'sneakin' around about a mile upstream from the shoals. Where there's one, there's bound to be more. I'm ridin' around to warn folks in the area. You might be well advised to stay over at Fort Watauga tonight," said the man.

"Thank you kindly, Mr. Finchum," replied Landon. "We will head that way."

The group began to make their way toward the fort, which was less than a mile away. Both Annabelle's father and uncle carried a rifle. It seemed to Cody as if this was a well-practiced drill. The only conversation that took place on the short walk came from Landon. He walked and spoke like a man who was feeling defeated. "I am afraid we aren't going to be able to stand up to much more of this," he said. "It is a miracle that we have withstood so many assaults as it is. If only we had gotten the needed votes to be added to the United States, we would have much better protection, federal protection. We were so close."

Cody understood now what Landon meant. As an independent state on the isolated western frontier, Franklin was vulnerable and exposed to all manner of assaults by Indians. As he considered this, the fort came into view. By now it was a familiar sight to Cody, since he had just experienced the Cherokee raids there in 1776. It looked very much the same, only the logs of the palisades had turned gray over the years, and there were a few more outbuildings.

It was apparent that most of the Watauga settlers had received the warning about the Indians in the vicinity. No one seemed overly concerned. In fact, it looked a bit like a social gathering. Cody saw little groups of men talking here and little groups of women there, and then his eyes caught sight of another group gathering inside the walls of the fortification. It was a small group of young people, most of whom appeared to be in their teens. There were, by Cody's quick count, four girls and three boys gathered.

One of the girls saw Cody and waved him over. "Hello, Annie!" she said. "It seems like the only time we get to see each other is when we are called into the fort on account of Indians. I wish things would settle down, and they would be able to build us a proper school."

Cody wasn't sure what to say, but he nodded in agreement.

"Papa says that we are going to have to give in and rejoin North Carolina soon," the girl went on. "Perhaps that will be good for us. Maybe that will give us the stability we need."

Cody knew not all the settlers felt like the girl's father. "I don't know," he replied. "My Uncle Landon tells me that North Carolina isn't very pleased with us and never has been all that supportive."

Cody suddenly had a very strange feeling that he was being watched. He slowly turned to steal a glance over his right shoulder. Sure enough, just as he looked, he saw one of the teenage boys shyly turn away as if he had been caught staring.

"I see you noticed James Talbot's attention," said the girl. "He is sweet on you, you know. We overheard him telling the other boys as you were walking this way."

State of North Carolina

By his Excellency Alexander Martin Esquire, Governor Captain General and Commander in chief of the said State.

To the Inhabitants of the Counties of Washington, Sullivan, and Greene.

A Manifesto.

Whereas I have received Letters from Brigadier General Sevier, under the style and Character of Governor; and from Mess'rs Landon Carter and William Cage, as speakers of the Senate and Commons of the State of Franklin; inform-ing me, that they with you the Inhabitants of part of the territory late ceded to Congress, had declared themselves independent of the State of North Carolina, and no longer considered themselves under the soveriegnty and jurisdiction of the same; Stating their reasons for their seperation and revolt; among

84

North Carolina Governor Alexander Martin issued a manifesto condemning the establishment of the state of Franklin in 1785. The first page of the manifesto includes the names of John Sevier and Landon Carter.

Now, this is too much, thought Cody. His worst fears about this journal now were beginning to be played out before him.

Then things got even worse, as Cody sensed James approaching him. "H-H-Hello Annie," James managed to stutter out nervously, unable to make direct eye contact. "It's n-n-nice to see you. That is a real p-p-pretty d-dress."

Oh, brother, this guy is really smooth, thought Cody, although he could relate well to James's nervousness, having never been very comfortable talking to girls himself. Still, he thought Annie would probably be polite.

"Good evening, James," Cody replied. "It's so nice to see you again." Cody really wanted to tell the boy to get lost.

"I-I was w-wondering if you would like to go for a walk with me sometime, maybe do a little fishing?" James nervously inquired.

"That sounds like fun," Cody replied, wanting to cut out his tongue before he could say anything else that might get him deeper into this hole.

James blushed and returned awkwardly to his friends, who, Cody could tell, began to immediately poke fun at him. It was a scene Cody had been a part of many times at school, only now he found himself on the opposite side of it. Cody turned back around to join the other girls.

"Annie, you are so lucky," said one of the other two girls. "James Talbot is just about the most handsome boy in the Watauga settlements." The other girls giggled in embarrassment.

"Oh, now stop it," Cody retorted. "He only asked me to go fishing!"

With that, all the girls burst out in laughter. Cody felt sick. *Ugh, if my friends could see me now*, he thought.

Cody was relieved to hear Landon calling to him. "Annie, did you want to continue our little history lesson?" Landon asked.

"Yes, let's," said Cody eagerly. He followed Landon into one of several little cabins built into the inside walls of the fort. It was a single room with bunks built into the walls and a table and chairs in the middle. He noticed several small holes cut into the outside wall of the cabin, holes just large enough to peer out of and perhaps stick a gun barrel through. He recognized it as the meeting room where Landon had sat with his father, John, and John Sevier on the day the report came of the Indian attacks on Eaton's Station back in 1776.

Landon pulled out a chair for Cody to sit in, then sat across the table from him.

"I don't expect too much to come of this," Landon said. "This doesn't feel like a raid to me. It's probably just a small scouting party or maybe a hunting party. But it is better to be safe than sorry. This little fort has protected the settlers in these parts from some pretty big Indian raids before. We'll be safe here."

"The last we talked, we left off with Franklin failing to get the two-thirds majority of the states to vote in favor of us joining the Union," Cody said.

"Right," replied Landon. "Well, there wasn't much we could do at that point; the votes were counted, and we were short. The delegates returned home, and we were left with some big decisions to make. Since we had seceded from North Carolina, we had no real protection from Indian attack, save whatever militia we could muster for ourselves. The legislature was elected. Officially, we met for the first time, in Greeneville, in December of 1785. You know a lot of the leaders of the government. Of course, John Sevier was governor, I was speaker of the Senate, and your friend James Talbot's father, Thomas, was clerk."

As Landon made that last remark about James Talbot, he had paused at the word "friend" and gave a sly little wink that made Cody feel embarrassed and angry.

Landon continued. "We got as much accomplished as we could over the next months. We worked out a couple of treaties with Indian tribes over land use. We set up a court system to handle cases of those accused of crimes. But there were many challenges that we had a hard time overcoming—and we still haven't found a way. We just don't have enough of an economy established to get a good foothold. As you know, we don't even have any official currency. We accept all manner of things for barter. Tobacco, corn, whiskey, deer hides, and even foreign currency are traded for items. Even Governor Sevier is paid in bucks. It's not the best way to grow your economy. It has been hard for us to overcome these challenges."

There it was again, thought Cody, *bucks*. The governor was paid in deerskins instead of money. Cody could understand how an economy based on this system would be hard pressed to compete with better-established governments with real treasuries.

"I fully support Governor Sevier," Landon continued. "He and his wife, Bonnie Kate, have been some of my dearest friends for many years." *So John Sevier ended up marrying the woman he saved from the Indians*, Cody realized.

"He is a man who has been caught up in circumstances that were beyond his control. His intentions have been nothing but the best from the beginning," Landon went on. "But North Carolina was not going to stand by and let us just up and leave without trying to get us back. They still claimed sovereignty over us and still expected us to pay taxes to them as well. To enforce this, they sent some military over the mountains to convince us that we had made a big mistake. Colonel John Tipton led troops over here, and that was what all

Colonel John Tipton (1730–1813) was against the establishment of the state of Franklin and led the rallying cry in 1787 for its return to North Carolina sovereignty.

INDIANA HISTORICAL SOCIETY

the fighting was about back in February of this year. Folks around here call it the Battle of Franklin. The battle broke out between Tipton's North Carolina troops and Sevier's Franklin militia. Tipton's army was just too large. It is the only battle that John Sevier ever lost, as far as I know."

"At any rate, that just left us even weaker. These continued Indian scares certainly don't help matters, either. Governor Sevier felt trapped between a rock and a hard place. He felt he had no place else to turn, so he met with representatives from Spain and tried to arrange for a loan. Some people loyal to

North Carolina also claimed he inquired about Franklin coming under control of the Spanish government, but I don't think that was ever seriously considered by either side. North Carolina ordered that Governor Sevier be arrested for treason. He turned himself in. Thankfully, the authorities were lenient with him, and he was released after swearing allegiance to North Carolina."

"Well, Annie, that brings us up to date. It looks certain that within the coming months, we will be forced to rejoin North Carolina—we simply have no other choice. We have tried to make a go of it alone, but it has proven to be unworkable," finished Landon.

As Landon completed his history, Cody felt himself being pulled out of the journal. When he opened his eyes, he was back in his bedroom.

Cody sat thinking back about this most recent journal experience. It had been a strange trip, but he was glad to have learned of the state of Franklin, even if he had to wear a dress to learn it.

Going over to his computer, Cody did a quick Internet search and found that indeed there once was a state of Franklin that later became the northeastern portion of Tennessee. Tennessee became a new state in 1796, just eight years after Cody had been there. He also learned that his grandfather's farm, in Hawkins County, would have been a part of the state of Franklin, if it had continued to exist.

Part Five

The Journal of Martin Carter
Fort Knox (Vincennes), Indiana Territory, 1811

11

The next several days were busy ones for Cody. He had little spare time for reading, and, truth be told, after his unnerving experience as a girl in the last journal, he was ready for a break. School occupied most of Cody's thoughts as he was being bombarded daily with review work.

In Mr. Foster's history class on Monday, the review assignment was to write an essay on any topic from the list of those that would be covered on the final exam. Cody looked over the list and saw a topic called the "American Spirit of Independence." Something immediately told him that was the topic he should choose to write about.

Cody got out some paper and a pen, and before he even realized it, he had begun writing. The words trailing from the end of Cody's pen seemed to be flowing from a stream of consciousness that he had little control over—it was as if he was simply reading the words as they appeared before him.

His essay began with an explanation of how America was started by people who were inherently distrustful of governments—people who valued their freedom above all else. He wrote about the Pilgrims and Puritans and the struggles they had in trying to worship God in the way that they wanted to. He wrote of how they ultimately decided to risk everything and uproot themselves to make a perilous three-thousand-mile journey west across a raging ocean to a strange wilderness filled with hardships and danger just to have an opportunity for the freedoms they sought. Their spirit of independence, wrote Cody, traveled with them every mile.

Cody continued his essay by detailing how independence and freedom were valued as the American colonies grew and expanded. He wrote of the colonists' continued cautious attitudes when it came to government control. He wrote that while the distance in miles between the mother country, England, and her American offspring did not change over the generations, the mental and emotional distance grew wider and wider with each passing year. He pointed out that Americans began to see themselves as a separate entity. He argued that the English king's failure to offer them a representative voice in their own government had only helped strengthen the colonists' independent spirit and drive them to become more unified.

Cody went on to detail the events that had caused the American spirit of independence to grow—the French and Indian War, the Proclamation of 1763, the Stamp Act, the Sugar Act, the Townshend Acts, the Boston Massacre, the Tea Act, the Boston Tea Party, the Intolerable Acts, among others—all of which were done without Americans having any official say about any of it. As Cody put it, the always-present spirit of independence in America was fertilized so much over the years by the short-sighted British government's actions that it grew out of control, and by 1776 it bore fruit in the form of the Declaration of Independence.

Cody wrote about how the spirit of independence did not fade even after the war for independence was won. Then he described in great detail the story of the state of Franklin. He told of a group of people who had risked everything to uproot themselves and travel hundreds of miles west across towering, mountainous wilderness into a strange land filled with hardships and danger just to have an opportunity for the freedoms they sought. In their fight to maintain their independence, they had failed, but their story was the same at the heart of it—Americans have always had a spirit of independence.

When Cody had finished his essay, he was surprised to see that he had more than doubled Mr. Foster's two-page length requirement. He had never been the type to go beyond what he was supposed to do on an assignment. Strangely, he didn't even really remember putting any real effort into his essay. As he read it back to himself, it seemed like someone else had written it. It sounded good in his head as he read silently—really good. When the bell rang, signaling the end of the period, and Cody turned in his essay, he noticed that most of the other kids in the class had barely filled one side of their paper.

The next morning at school, Mr. Foster flagged down Cody in the hall and motioned for him to come and see him. Cody followed the teacher into his classroom and sat down.

"Cody, I just wanted to talk to you about the essay you wrote yesterday. I wanted to tell you that I am most impressed," Mr. Foster said. "The way you laid out the facts about how America has always had a spirit of independence was excellent. You cited all the right things that drove America towards a Declaration of Independence and a war for independence. It was all done very well. I was not surprised that you were able to explain that. I was surprised by something, however."

Uh oh, thought Cody. *Am I in some sort of trouble? Does he think I cheated somehow, or plagiarized?*

"The end of your essay was most interesting to me," continued his teacher. "The way you paralleled the story of the state of Franklin with the beginning of your essay about the Pilgrims and Puritans was not only very well done, it was also news to me. I have a master's degree and have been teaching many years, yet I've never heard the story of the state of Franklin. Where did you learn about this?"

Cody almost started telling his teacher how he traveled back in time and entered the bodies of his long-dead teenage ancestors. Just as he was about to do it, he stopped himself. *I can't tell him that*, he thought. *He'll think I'm nuts. He would probably march me right down to the office and have me tested for drugs!* Cody paused a moment and decided to play it safe.

"I have family roots in that area," Cody answered. "My grandfather lives in Hawkins County, Tennessee. He gave me some information to read, and I learned that area was a part of the state of Franklin. When I found out about that, I just started doing some more research about it. I thought it was cool that there was a whole state once that I hadn't even heard of and that some of my family is from there."

"I agree. I think it is cool, too," said Mr. Foster. "I'll let you get going so you won't be late to class. I just wanted to compliment you on your excellent essay, and thank you for teaching something new to your old history teacher."

Cody thanked his teacher and headed off to math class with a little extra bounce in his step.

On Friday night, after a busy week, Cody decided to sit down and start reading the next journal in his time line. He opened the old book and saw the title page: *The Journal of Martin Carter . . . Indiana Territory . . . 1811.* He felt a cold chill run down his spine. He recalled that his dad had mentioned his one journal experience, the one that he could not handle, had taken place in the Indiana Territory. Was this the journal that had shaken up his father years ago? What kind of experience could have caused his dad to give up on the entire family tradition? Unsettled, Cody was tempted to skip this journal and go to the next one, but he realized that he just had to know. Plus, he had just a touch of obsessive–compulsiveness that drove him to do things in the proper order. To leave this chronology at this point, he knew, would only drive him batty. No, he decided, he simply must forge ahead.

Overlooking the Wabash River near Vincennes, Indiana, Fort Knox consisted of a few build-ings surrounded by a palisade fence. The fort provided American settlers with protection as tensions increased between them and the Native Americans just before the War of 1812.

He nervously turned the page and began to read.

My name is Martin Carter. I am fourteen years old. I live near Fort Knox, along the banks of the Wabash River in the Indiana Territory. My mother died of smallpox before I was two years old. I live with my father, Samuel. He works as an aide and adviser for Governor William Harrison. . . .

As he read these words, Cody once again felt the familiar swimming sensation in his head and the butterflies dancing in his stomach. When he opened his eyes, he was standing outside a large brick home. The house was impressive, with white columns bracketing a stately two-story front porch. One end of the house was rounded with paneled windows and black shutters. Nearby, on Cody's left, flowed a large river.

Cody saw a man motion to him from the front porch of the large house. Cody began to walk toward the house, and the man spoke. "Come, Martin, I have a message for you to deliver to your father," the man said.

"Y-y-yes, sir," replied Cody uncertainly.

Cody suddenly realized he must be standing before Governor William Henry Harrison. Who else would have such a fine house as this? Cody was visualizing a mental checklist of the famous people he had now met—Daniel Boone . . . check; Dragging Canoe . . . check; John Sevier . . . check; Governor (and future president) William Henry Harrison . . . check—unbelievable!

When Cody reached the steps of the porch, the man was reaching into a pocket inside his jacket. He removed an envelope and handed it to Cody. "Take this to your father. Tell him that I am arranging a meeting of my staff. It is all explained in the letter."

Cody looked at the envelope. It was sealed closed with a dollop of wax that had been stamped with Governor Harrison's seal. "I will take it to him straight away, sir," Cody said.

"Thank you, Martin," Harrison replied.

But which way to go to find Martin's father? Cody knew from the journal that Martin's family lived along the Wabash River, so he decided to follow the river and see where it led. After a short distance, he drew near a modest frame house. As he approached, a man exited the front door and greeted him. "Hello, son!"

Cody was relieved. The man must be Samuel Carter. "I have a message from the governor," he said.

Built in 1804, this two-story brick house was home to Governor William Henry Harrison and his family in Vincennes, Indiana, through the end of the War of 1812. This photo, ca. mid- to late-1800s, shows the house very much as it looked in 1811.

"Let's have it then," said Samuel. They entered the house, and Samuel took the note to a writing desk near a window in the far corner of the room.

"Governor Harrison says he needs you to come to a meeting," Cody said. "What is it about?"

"Calm down there, son," Samuel replied. "I haven't even had time to open this yet."

Cody watched as the man carefully broke the seal and unfolded the note. After reading for a moment, Samuel spoke again. "Harrison says Tecumseh has gone south and left his brother in charge at Tippecanoe. He says he wants to discuss a plan he has to take advantage of Tecumseh's absence. We will meet tomorrow morning."

Suddenly, Cody felt his head swimming once again and sensed everything beginning to go dark. A curtain seemed to open before him, and he found himself back in his bedroom. He sat there for a moment mulling over what he had just been through. "I met one of the presidents of the United States," he muttered in disbelief. "Of course, he hadn't been president yet, but still. . . ." Cody wondered what traumatic event might be awaiting him in this journal. Something in it had disturbed his dad—that was for sure—but what?

12

Cody was very intrigued with this new journal for a couple of reasons. First, there was the issue of whatever it was that lay ahead that had disturbed his father so much. That unknown was hanging like a thick fog in Cody's brain. He was more than a little nervous about it. This whole journal had a rather ominous feel to it anyway, for reasons that Cody couldn't put his finger on yet. Though the unknown prospects of this journal were more than a little frightening, they were also exciting. The adventurer's fire deep inside of Cody had been stoked a great deal since he had first begun this exercise. He had been through enough now to make him think he could stand up in the face of anything the journals could throw at him. He was ready to move ahead—or at least he had convinced himself that he was ready.

Since it was still rather early on a Friday night, he decided to dive right back in. He found the next entry in the journal and began to read.

I was hunting along the Wabash a couple miles upriver from Governor Harrison's mansion, Grouseland, when I ran across my Shawnee friend Sitting Fox. . . .

Cody's head swam and the butterflies danced in his stomach. When he came to, he was standing by a river holding a rifle. He was wearing buckskin clothing, and he stood face to face with a half-naked Indian boy who appeared to be about the same age as Martin, probably fourteen or fifteen. The boy wore buckskin leggings but was shirtless. The boy was strikingly handsome. His face was narrow with sharp features, and his eyes were almost coal black and perfectly symmetrical. His jet-black hair was pulled tightly back into a ponytail that swung down between his shoulder blades. The boy was holding not a gun but a bow, and a quiver full of arrows was slung over his left shoulder. Around the boy's neck hung a leather necklace from which hung a small beaded pouch.

Cody knew this must be Sitting Fox. "Hello, Sitting Fox," he said.

"Martin, it does me good to see you," said Sitting Fox. "For the past two moons I have been with a hunting party led by my brother, Long Bow. We are returning now from the area where the Beautiful River flows into the Father of the Waters. I separated myself from the rest of the party so that I might come and see you. Soon, I must hurry off and rejoin my party as we return to Tenskwatawa's village on the Tippecanoe-se-pe."

Cody realized that "se-pe" must mean river—sort of like Missis-*si-ppi*. He remembered that the Mississippi River had been called "Father of the Waters" by some native people. Was the "Beautiful River" Sitting Fox mentioned the Ohio River, which flowed into the Mississippi?

"How was the hunting?" he asked Sitting Fox.

"We did not have the success we had hoped for. The settlers in Cain-tuck-ee have killed much of the game that once was so plentiful there. That is why we went farther toward the setting sun in search of game. Even in those lands, we saw many signs of the settlers' presence. I can tell you, Martin my brother, my people are not happy. My brother speaks much of the treaties of your Chief Harrison. He says the treaties are worthless. He says that the Indians give up much, and the white man gives up little, then the white man just takes more and makes a new treaty, each more worthless than the last. Our great Chief Tecumseh says there will be no treaty with his name upon it. He goes now into the lands far below Cain-tuck-ee—to the lands of our fathers. He goes to unite all the Indian tribes to stand against Chief Harrison. Tecumseh says he has tried to come to the peace council and reason with your chief, but he will not listen. I fear, my brother, that a great war will be upon us soon."

"I wish our people could get along as you and I do," said Cody.

"My heart fears that it is too late for that, my brother," replied Sitting Fox.

Cody was quiet for a moment, looking at his friend. He noticed a necklace Sitting Fox was wearing. "What is that pouch that hangs around your neck?" he asked.

"That is my *pa-waw-ka*. This pouch holds the symbol of my passage to man-hood. I will wear it until the day that I die," answered Sitting Fox.

"What is your *pa-waw-ka*? When did you get it? Who gave it to you?" Cody said.

"No one gave it to me. I had to earn it," said Sitting Fox, as he opened the little beaded pouch and pulled out a small, shiny stone. "To you, this looks like a stone, but to me, and to my people, it is much more. It represents my inner fire. I had to suffer much to earn my *pa-waw-ka*. Each morning for four

Tecumseh (1768–1813), a Shawnee warrior, met with Governor William Henry Harrison on several occasions to discuss the United States' forced removal of Native American tribes westward. Tecumseh and his brother Tenskwatawa, also known as the Prophet, organized a large alliance from many different tribes to stand against the Americans.

Tecumseh's speech to Governor Harrison 20th Aug 1810

Brother, I wish you to listen to me well – I wish to reply to you more explicitly – as I think you do not clearly understand what I before said to you I shall explain it again –

When we were first discovered it was by the French who told us that they would adopt us as their children and gave us presents, without asking any thing in return but merely considering them as our Fathers – Since we have changed our fathers we find it different –

Bro. This is the manner that the treaty was made by us with the French, they gave us many presents & treated us well they asked us for a small piece of country to live on which they were not to leave and continue to treat us as their children after some time the British & French came to quarrel the British were victorious yet the French promised to think of us as their child & if they ever could serve us to do it – now my red children I know I was obliged to abandon you in a disagreeable circumstances, but we have never ceased to look upon you & if we could now be of service to you we would stile be your friends,

The next father we found was the British who told us that they would now be our fathers and treat us in the same manner as our former fathers the French – they would occupy the same land they did & not trouble us on ours, but would look on us as their children –

Bro. We were very glad to hear the British promise to treat us our fathers the French had done they began to treat us in the same way, but at last they changed their good treatment by raising the Tomhawk against the Americans & put it into our hands, by which we have suffered the loss of a great many of our young men &c –

In this speech to Governor William Henry Harrison, Tecumseh states that the killing of Native Americans in America's ruthless pursuit of their lands would no longer be tolerated.

moons I had to get up before dawn, strip naked, and plunge myself into the cold waters of the Tippecanoe-se-pe. All Shawnee warriors must endure this. It is always done in the months when the snow flies. Earning a *pa-waw-ka* is supposed to be very hard to do. There were many mornings when I did not think I would live through it—mornings when I had to break through thick ice with a club and tomahawk just to be able to go into the water below. The coldest of all was the final day, when I was permitted to finally grab up my *Pa-waw-ka*. On that morning, I was led to the river. Other men had broken open a hole in the ice, and I was told that I must jump into the water four times on that day. On the fourth dive, I went all the way to the bottom and retrieved my *pa-waw-ka*."

"Did someone place it there for you to find?" asked Cody.

"No man did. No one knows what a young man's *pa-waw-ka* will be. The Great Spirit, Weshemoneto, provides each young man's *pa-waw-ka*. We must dive to the bottom and scoop up whatever he provides. This is what I scooped up that morning—this is my *pa-waw-ka*," said Sitting Fox, holding up the shiny black stone. "This is the essence of who I am. No man can take this from me. I can brave the fiercest battle, last through starving times, even stay warm in the coldest winter, because I have my *pa-waw-ka*."

"It's beautiful," said Cody.

Cody could hardly imagine having to go through such an ordeal as Sitting Fox had just described. The very thought of getting up before dawn every morning through four months of bitter cold winter and dunking yourself into an ice-cold river—all for a chance at a rock to carry around your neck. On the surface, the whole idea seemed silly. Yet, something deep inside Cody could not help but feel envious. There was nothing at all like this in his own culture. He thought it would be very cool to have something like that to accomplish in order to become a man.

For the next couple of hours, the friends talked and laughed, swam in the Wabash, and attempted in vain to shoot fish with Sitting Fox's bow and arrow. Then Sitting Fox suddenly became serious again.

"The hour grows late; I must hurry off and rejoin my brother and the hunting party. He would not be happy with me if he knew I was here, so near Chief Harrison's village. He does not understand my friendship with you—I cannot make him understand."

Cody could feel Sitting Fox's sadness. "Perhaps one day our people will find a common ground and live in harmony," he said.

"I pray that day will come," answered Sitting Fox.

With that, the young Indian was off like a flash, heading north toward his village. As he watched Sitting Fox bound off into the distance, Cody suddenly felt the return of the swimming sensation in his head. The next thing he knew, he was back in his bedroom.

Cody remembered that his history textbook mentioned Tecumseh, so he picked up the book and thumbed through it. He learned that Tenskwatawa was better known to the whites as "The Prophet" and was the younger brother of the great Shawnee leader Tecumseh. He read that The Prophet was a spiritual leader who preached to the Shawnee that they needed to turn away from their dependence on the white man's ways.

Cody wondered how much Sitting Fox agreed with the teachings of Tenskwatawa. He had genuinely liked Sitting Fox. He hated that the white settlers and the Indians were having such troubles. He even found himself longing for a *pa-waw-ka* of his own. He wasn't at all sure he liked where this journal seemed to be heading.

13

Cody had a fitful night's sleep. He tossed and turned, drifting between dream-filled stints of restless sleep and frustrating periods when he stared at his bedroom ceiling deep in nagging thoughts. He had felt the closeness between Martin Carter and Sitting Fox, and that meant he felt as if Sitting Fox was *his* friend. He also sensed the uneasiness of their relationship—the forbidden nature of it.

Cody was not so naïve to think that he lived in perfect times where everyone got along. He realized that there was still racism and bigotry in his twenty-first century world. He understood that people still sometimes had difficulty seeing eye-to-eye when cultures clashed. Yet, in his day-to-day life, things seemed to be much more civil than all of this. On any given day at school, Cody hung out with kids from different cultural backgrounds. He had friends who were African American, Asian, and Hispanic. He even had friends who claimed to have Native American ancestry. Everyone seemed to be able to find enough common ground to get along and be friends.

So why did Martin Carter and Sitting Fox have such a challenging friendship? Why, in 1811, did it seem so impossible for two boys just to hang out together and be friends? Cody could not get his mind around these questions. The whole situation frustrated him. He wanted to be able to do something about it.

Cody was also thinking about what Sitting Fox had said about his *pa-waw-ka*. The more he thought about it, the more it intrigued him. What had, at first blush, seemed a silly and pointless ritual now seemed to make ultimate sense to him. Cody lay there in his bed wishing there was something that he could put himself through to prove that he was worthy of being a man—a warrior! The more he thought about it, the more the idea appealed to him—putting yourself through a test of mental and physical endurance, after which you have something to keep with you forever. Cody wondered if he would ever have anything like that. He longed to discover and know his inner fire.

After what seemed like hours, Cody finally drifted off to sleep. He awoke at eight o'clock, feeling less than refreshed. He decided to grab a quick breakfast and get right back into the Martin Carter journal. After scarfing down a couple of toaster pastries and a glass of milk, he headed back to his room and sat down to read.

November 8, 1811—The report from my father is very worrisome. Upon hearing the news that Tenskwatawa (the Prophet) has been mobilizing warriors along the Tippecanoe River, Governor Harrison was called back from Kentucky, where he had been on business. Tecumseh is currently away in the lands far to the south trying to organize a coalition of tribes to support his cause. He shows all signs of preparing for war. Even after meeting at Grouseland with Governor Harrison earlier this year and vowing his peaceful intentions, he has gone again to rally more warriors from faraway tribes to his cause. Tecumseh has shown that he does not respect any of the treaties that Governor Harrison has developed with the Indians of the territory. His hatred of the treaties goes all the way back to when I was just a baby—when the treaty of Fort Wayne gave Harrison more than three million acres for the Indiana Territory. Tecumseh even threatens to seek an alliance with the British if such treaties are allowed to continue. He takes great pride in saying that no treaty will ever bear his name. He claims that Harrison has no right to make treaties with one tribe of Indians when the lands belong to all tribes. A few weeks ago, Governor Harrison took armed troops toward Prophetstown. Along the way, supplies ran low and they built a small fort and awaited the arrival of replenishments. Once they received their provisions, they continued their march, and I was sent to join my father here at the fort. As Governor Harrison marches toward Prophetstown, the hope is that this show of force will convince the Prophet and his followers that peace is their only option. I wonder if a show of force is really the way to bring lasting peace. I worry about my friend, Sitting Fox. . . .

Reading these words, Cody felt himself once again being drawn into the journal. The next thing he knew, he was sitting inside the walls of a small fort, watching a rider on horseback gallop in through the open gates. As the rider grew closer, Cody realized he was Martin's father, Samuel.

Samuel pulled back on the reigns to stop his horse and dismounted. "Martin, I have news from Prophetstown," he said.

This etching of the Battle of Tippecanoe depicts Governor William Henry Harrison saddled on his horse with his arm outstretched, sword in hand, while leading his men to victory over Tenskwatawa, the Prophet.

"Has there been a battle?" Cody asked impatiently, feeling concerned for Sitting Fox.

"Here is what I know," replied Samuel. "Two days ago, as our forces got nearer to Prophetstown, they were approached by an Indian rider waving a white flag. He carried a message from the Prophet requesting a cease-fire until a peace council could be arranged. Harrison didn't trust the Prophet's motives, but he agreed to meet the next day."

Cody felt a flood of relief at the possibility this may have ended with no bloodshed. He let out a deep breath.

Samuel continued. "Harrison moved his troops to high ground near where the Tippecanoe empties into the Wabash. He had his men on full alert and battle ready. Yesterday morning, well before first light, the camp was awakened by gunshots."

Cody felt his heart sink as he began to realize that this standoff was probably not going to have a peaceful conclusion.

"Apparently, during the night, the Prophet had sent warriors to sneak in and kill Governor Harrison," Samuel went on. "They had encircled some of the sentries outside the camp. Just as shots were fired on that end of the camp, fierce fighting began to break out on the other end. Governor Harrison's mistrust of the Prophet's peace request was well founded. For the next few hours, the fighting raged on. We are still trying to get accurate casualty counts, but it is clear that we lost a good many men. About the time the sun rose, the Indians seemed to be running low on ammunition, as their shots became fewer. With the light of day, it must have become obvious to them that they were severely outnumbered. Our troops organized one last push and drove the Indians away. At last count, we had nearly forty confirmed dead from this attack and more than twenty others that are certain to be mortally wounded."

"What are the Indian casualties?" Cody asked nervously.

"We don't know. There were a good many of them, too—maybe not as many as we suffered, but our preliminary count estimates a few dozen Indian dead and a few more than that wounded," Samuel said.

With those words, Cody felt a surge of fear and adrenaline race through his veins. Had Sitting Fox been among those casualties? He ran toward a horse that was hitched to a post nearby. He leapt up and straddled the animal, freed the reigns from the post, wheeled around, and started through the gates at full gallop. He could hear Samuel shouting something to him in the background, but he ignored the words and sped on.

Cody had never ridden a horse at such speeds before. He tore across the countryside headed in the direction from which Samuel had come. He could feel the wind in his face, and he encouraged the horse to keep running and to run even faster. He felt the stinging whips of low-hanging twigs and branches as he rode through the woods. He felt the cold splash of water on his legs and chest as he plunged through creeks. He had no way of knowing for sure if he was going in the right direction.

Time meant nothing on Cody's blinding ride. Before he knew it, he could see some soldiers up ahead, and he slowed the horse. The soldiers seemed to be walking around searching for something. Some were squatting down examining things on the ground. Others were holding rifles, sitting atop horses and scanning the surrounding horizons. As he rode closer, Cody began to make out more details. He could see that the men were taking inventory of the fallen men from the battle that had raged here the day before.

Cody felt nauseous as he looked on the macabre scene before him. To his left was a flatbed wagon being loaded with the uniformed bodies of dead soldiers who had served under General Harrison. There looked to be more than a dozen bodies on this one wagon. An identical wagon was much farther away, and it appeared to have a similar cargo. The men who were investigating the scene now were making notes about the fallen Indians still laying all around the area.

Unable to stop himself, Cody climbed down from the horse. He began to slowly walk around. He glanced up and noticed another grisly sight in the sky. Dozens of buzzards had begun circling. Cody felt sick to his stomach, but he continued walking toward one of the men who was investigating a fallen Indian.

"Son, what are you doin' here?" said the soldier. "This is no place fer a boy yer age."

"I am looking for someone," Cody replied coldly. He took a long look at the fallen warrior in front of him. The man had been shot through the chest, and his entire torso was stained with blackish-red dried blood. The Indian's face was painted half red and half black. His lifeless eyes were still wide open. The soldiers had taken the weapons from the Indian's body, and Cody guessed that was what they were writing down in their notebooks. He noticed there was a little bag hanging on a necklace around the Indian's neck. His *pa-waw-ka* had remained with him until the day he died.

"What will become of the bodies of the fallen Indians?" asked Cody.

"I don't rightly know," answered the soldier. "I reckon their kin will return for the bodies once we leave—or the buzzards and coyotes'll get 'em. It don't make no difference to me one way 'r 'nother. We're just here to count 'em and salvage any weapons we can."

Cody felt a churning heat rising in his belly and turned away from the scene. He trotted quickly toward a little grove of trees as his throat grew tight and he broke into a cold sweat. When he reached the tree line, he dropped to all fours and began to heave and wretch violently. It was as if all the fear and sorrow he had ever felt was erupting from his guts in one putrid gush. Finally, when he could heave no more, Cody slowly returned to his feet to continue his search.

As he walked around the area, Cody came upon several other scenes very similar to the one that had made him sick, yet he seemed numb now. He still felt profound sadness, but it was as if he was outside his body, watching himself go through the motions of this search.

Then Cody saw something that brought him fully back into the moment. About twenty yards in front of him was a familiar form. He felt his heart sink

The Battle of Tippecanoe
(from *Indiana Journal*, August 6, 1836)

Air – *Star-Spangled Banner*
No voice broke the silence—no breath stirred the
air,
And the moon on the white tents shown wan
as with sorrow;
The worn soldiers slept—but their chieftain stood
there,
And watched by his war-steed and thought of
the morrow.
His soul-lighted eye, was upraised to the
sky—
'In the dread hour of battle, Oh God be
thou nigh—
And teach us—to thee and our country still
true—
To conquer or perish at Tippecanoe!'

But hark! there's a foot-step falls faint on the
ear,
'Tis the sentinel's tread, for he only is waking;
Again! Now a shot! Ha! the Indian is here;
Up! Up! And to arms! At the hero's command,
Each stern brow was knit, and each bold heart
was ready;
Up-starting their tried weapons grasped in each hand,
'A volley! Now charge boys! Be steady—be
steady!
Their chief he was there—amid thunder and
glare,
The fierce shout of triumph—the shriek of
despair,
Undaunted, the foremost to dare and to do,
The bravest, the noblest at Tippecanoe!

They triumphed—how nobly, let history tell,—
Be honor to those who for freedom contended!
Let our shouts with the proud name of Harrison
swell,
Who our liberty shielded—our country
defended.
The laurel and song—to the hero belong,
Who ne'er lost a battle, and ne'er did a
wrong.
Then conquer for him who has conquered
for you—
And huzza for the hero of Tippecanoe!
R. T. C.

As the twenty-fifth anniversary of the Battle of Tippecanoe neared in 1836, the Indiana
Journal *reprinted the poem, "The Battle of Tippecanoe." The poem celebrates Governor
William Henry Harrison's victory over the Native Americans. Note how the last lines of the
poem cheer Harrison's accomplishment. Even today, the battlefield is preserved, so visitors
can walk the grounds where Harrison and the Prophet fought.*

with a terrible suspicion. The lifeless figure lying in the bloodstained weeds before him looked like Sitting Fox.

Cody felt like running away and hiding, but instead he ran toward the fallen young warrior. He knelt down and examined the corpse's face. It certainly looked like Sitting Fox, but severe damage from a head wound and war paint made it hard to be certain. Then Cody noticed the little beaded bag hanging around the young Indian's neck. It looked very much like that which Sitting Fox wore. Slowly, Cody reached for the bag and opened it. He emptied its contents into the palm of his hand and saw the shiny black stone—Sitting Fox's *pa-waw-ka*.

Cody's heart was filled with grief and despair. He squeezed the little rock tightly in his hand. He closed his eyes and felt a hot tear beginning to roll down his face. Just as he began to feel himself sob uncontrollably, he felt the swimming sensation returning in his head. When he opened his eyes, he was back in his bedroom. He should have felt relief, but he felt nothing but utter sorrow.

Cody ran to his bed and buried his face in his pillow. He had not cried like this for as long as he could remember, but he could not stop the tears from coming. He had never seen a dead body except for those in coffins at funeral homes. Somehow, death had never seemed so real to him. He knew that he would never forget the looks on the faces of those fallen Shawnee warriors. He would never forget the blood. He would never forget the contorted bodies frozen in their final pose of pain, or the buzzards circling in the sky. He would surely never forget the horrifying sight of his friend, Sitting Fox, lying there in the bloodstained weeds.

Then Cody was struck with a realization so real and strong that he thought it had been placed directly into his heart by some power he couldn't fully comprehend. Cody suddenly knew that he had just received his inner fire. He had earned his own *pa-waw-ka*.

PART SIX

The Journal of David Carter
Metamora, Indiana, 1846

14

Once again, Cody had emerged from a journal emotionally spent. This time, however, he felt like a different person. His *pa-waw-ka* experience had changed him. He had gone into Martin Carter's journal as a boy and come back as a young man—a warrior. This journey had left Cody with a much deeper understanding of the tenuous relationship between European Americans and Native Americans. He had known that they had come into conflict throughout the early history of America, but the textbooks mentioned major incidents that occurred here and there—and not in great detail. Cody had never experienced the strong sense of nearly constant tension and fear that existed on the frontier over the many years of westward expansion. He had never felt so emotionally invested in this part of history before now.

As Cody sat in his room, still choking back sobs when he thought of Sitting Fox's death, his mind wandered back to the horrible tale of the slaughter of Edward Carter's grandparents during the Tuscarora Wars in North Carolina. He remembered the attacks on Fort Watauga in the journals of Landon and Annabelle Carter. Even though some of his own family members had suffered through horrible times at the hands of Native Americans, he had a great deal of trouble sorting the whole story out. It would be easy for someone to react emotionally to the loss of family members in brutal attacks and feel resentment toward the attackers. Yet, Cody didn't sense any real animosity toward the Native Americans. It would also be easy for someone to look at the encroachment of white settlers into native lands and feel that the settlers got what was coming to them, but Cody didn't exactly feel that way either. The whole situation was too complex to comprehend completely.

Cody decided that the tragedy of the situation was that both sides were, in the end, just trying to make a life for themselves. The problem centered on the different cultures' concept of land ownership. To the Native Americans, the tradition of drawing imaginary lines and dividing lands by boundaries was completely foreign. To the Americans, the natives' idea that the land belonged to no one man or group and was for the use of everyone was childish and idealistic. The idea of private property was so deeply woven into the cultures of Europeans and Americans that it seemed to flow through the settlers' veins as a part of their life force. No treaty could have ever adequately bridged that gap.

It took a few days for Cody to feel ready to return to the journals. He was glad that he had decided to go through the journals chronologically. He wondered how he would have reacted if he had randomly started with Martin Carter's journal, like his father had done. Going through the experiences of the earlier journals first had slowly prepared Cody for the devastating tragedy of Sitting Fox. It didn't make it easy—it just prepared him for it. Although he certainly wouldn't want to go through an experience like that again, he felt it had been a valuable thing to take with him.

Meanwhile, it was Cody's last week of school. There were lots of final exams, but there were also lots of fun year-end activities. In history class, the final exam was to write a paper that told the story of America from the colonies to the Civil War. Thanks in part to his journal experiences, Cody wrote an excellent paper and received an A and a glowing note from his teacher.

By Friday night Cody was ready for his summer break and to start reading a new journal. He reached for the next journal in line and noticed that there were only two left. This one was labeled *The Journal of David Carter—Metamora, Indiana—1846*. He opened the journal and began to read.

> *My name is David Carter. I am sixteen years old. I live in the town of Metamora in Franklin County, Indiana. My parents are Oliver and Mary. We moved here from Kentucky in 1836, when my pa got hired as a canal worker. Now he is a lock tender on the Whitewater Canal. We live next to the lock in a little house that was furnished for us by the canal company. My mother sells baked goods to boat passengers. I have recently begun to help my father with the lock tending. We have to be on duty whenever boats come by on the canal, so Pa needs some breaks now and then. . . .*

As Cody read these words, he felt the familiar sensations that always accompanied his trips into the journals. When he opened his eyes this time, he found himself standing alongside a strange-looking stream of water. It would have looked like a creek, but it was too straight—too perfectly straight. This looked like a man-made creek. Cody realized it must be the Whitewater Canal.

The canal looked to be about forty to fifty feet wide. Along the sides were well-worn paths. Cody glanced around at his surroundings. He was in a little valley. It was a lovely spot. Tree-covered ridges towered above the valley floor, and a beautiful river flowed about three hundred feet behind him. Between the canal and the river was fairly level bottomland that had been plowed into farm fields. Just a few yards to his right sat a small house. Off in the distance, Cody could see a few houses and buildings.

Right in front of Cody was a complex structure built into the canal. He took a moment to study the situation. It looked like a stairway in the canal. There was a drop-off here of several feet in elevation. The stone and wood structure seemed to be framing a waterfall. There was a set of large gates at the top of the waterfall and another set down below it. Between the two gates was a large gap, and the walls in the gap were lined with stone. It created a long and deep chamber. Little side channels of water bypassed the main canal, and small gates stopped the water in the channels from flowing into the chamber between the larger gates.

As he was studying his surroundings, Cody was startled by a female voice. He turned to see a woman coming toward him. "David, darlin', your pa's gone to Metamora to the post office and wants you to tend the lock. He said there might be a boat comin' with a load of produce and a few passengers on their way to Brookville," she said.

So whatever this wooden contraption is, it must be called a "lock," thought Cody, and apparently, I am supposed to tend it . . . whatever that means.

"Here they come now," said the woman. Cody realized she must be Mary Carter, David's mother. "David, you've never operated the lock by yourself. Are you sure you can do it?"

Cody wasn't sure, but he replied as confidently as he could. "Y-yes. I've watched Pa do it hundreds of times."

"He left a note with instructions in your pocket, just in case," said Mary, smiling at him. "I have a batch of pies coolin' in the house. I best go fetch them and see if any of the passengers want to buy some."

As Mary turned toward the house, Cody reached into his pocket, found the instructions, and began to study them. When he was confident he understood the process, he looked up the canal and saw a long, narrow craft creeping along at a slow but steady pace. The boat was being pulled on a towrope by two horses that walked along the path paralleling the canal. He could see a few crates stacked on the deck of the boat and several people sitting on benches.

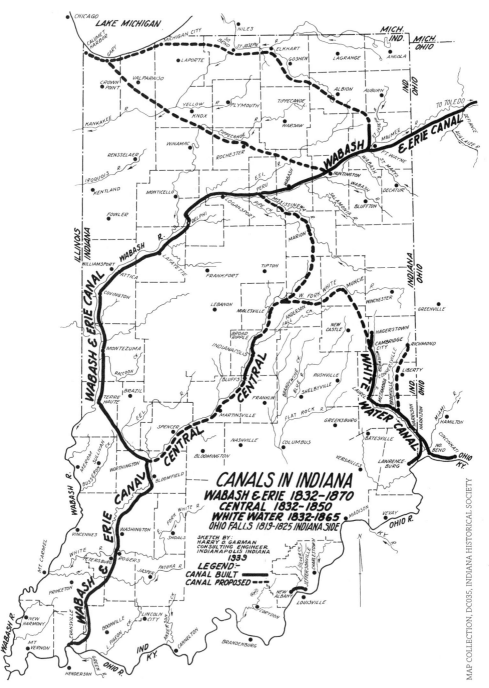

The Whitewater Canal, which flows through Metamora in Franklin County, is located in the eastern section of Indiana and runs northwest into the central part of the state. This map also shows the route of the Wabash and Erie Canal as well as the proposed routes of canals never completed.

He walked down to the lower gates of the lock and studied the mechanism, considering the instructions David's father had written. What had looked like a stair step in the canal was exactly that. The water level in the chamber could be raised or lowered to match the level of the canal. When the water level was even with the canal, the boat would pull into the chamber, and one set of gates would close behind it. Depending on the boat's direction of travel, the water then would be let out either into or out of the chamber. The boat would move with the water level until it was even with the level of the next section of the canal. It was a simple but ingenious device that allowed boats to go up and down hills.

Cody began to swing the gates closed. It was hard work, but he managed it. The gates fit together very snugly and effectively stopped almost all of the flow of water from escaping. Then he walked back and opened the little gates that blocked off the side channel and allowed water to flow into the rising waters behind the closed gates. Cody stood and watched the large chamber between the lock gates slowly fill with water. By the time the boat arrived, the water in the lock chamber was already at the top level of the canal. Cody closed the little gate that allowed the side channel water in, stopping any more water from entering. He watched as the boat operator maneuvered the craft into the chamber. When the boat was fully inside the lock chamber, Cody closed the upper gates behind it. Some of the passengers then got off the boat to stretch their legs and make use of the nearby outhouse. Meanwhile, Cody went to the lower set of gates and began to crack them open to allow some of the water in the chamber to slowly escape. The boat began to descend with the water level. It took about ten minutes for the boat to reach the lower level of the canal, and then Cody opened the lower gates all the way. The passengers began to reboard the boat. Cody noticed that three of them were carrying fresh pies they had purchased from Mary during their brief stop. Once all the passengers were back in their seats, the boat operator called for the horses to begin pulling again, and the boat slowly headed off to finish the last leg of the trip to Brookville.

Once the boat had left the lock, Cody went into the little house. "I see you sold some pies," he said to Mary.

"Yes, I only have two left. I'll send one with you to the dance tonight if you want," Mary replied. "Don't forget to write in the tender's log."

Cody looked around the room and noticed a little table just inside the door with a logbook sitting open upon it. Each entry in the book contained the name of the boat, the number of passengers, a description of the cargo, the time it arrived, and where it was going from there. He entered the information about the boat that had just passed through, then paused as Mary's words sunk in.

"The dance tonight?" Cody repeated.

"I can't believe you'd forget," Mary said teasingly. "It starts at six. But I'd clean up before you go." She gestured toward a small bedroom that opened off the main room of the house.

Cody entered the bedroom and found a suitable outfit in a dresser. He combed through his hair before returning to the main room.

"You look nice, dear," said Mary. "Such a handsome young man! Here is an apple pie to take with you."

"Thanks," Cody replied.

"Have fun, and don't go breakin' too many hearts," Mary said.

Cody felt himself blush with embarrassment at her teasing. "Don't worry," he said, as he grabbed the pie and headed out the door.

Cody decided to head toward the houses and buildings he had seen in the distance when he first arrived. The route took him along the same path that the horses had walked when they pulled the boat toward him on the canal. As he neared the little town, he saw a sign that read *Metamora, Indiana*. He walked on into the village. The canal went right through the middle of the town. There was a row of businesses on each side of the canal. Cody walked by a mercantile, a blacksmith, a hotel, a gristmill, a cobbler shop, a doctor's office, and several other little shops. A couple of streets were lined with houses, and a church sat at the end of one street. Ahead, outside a large building near the end of the main street, several young adults and teens mingled. They all seemed to be dressed in their Sunday-best clothing. Two teenage boys who were congregating near the front steps of the building greeted Cody as he came close to the building.

"Hello there, David," said a red-haired, freckle-faced young man.

"Howdy," Cody replied. "How is everything?"

"Pa has me workin' like a dog," he replied. "Ben here has it made as usual," he said, pointing to the tall, lanky blonde boy to his left. "He just goes fishin' every blessed day while his daddy runs the store."

"That would be nice, Joe, if it were true," said Ben, laughing. "Hey, Dave, did you hear about the new family that moved to town this week?"

Cody shook his head. "I've been busy."

"I hear tell they come from Pennsylvania. They came down the Ohio River to Cincinnati and then came over here to settle. I don't know too much about 'em except that they have a daughter that is our age. I saw her, and she is all

JACOB ABBOTT, *MARCO PAUL'S VOYAGES AND TRAVELS ON THE ERIE CANAL* (NEW YORK: HARPER AND BROTHERS, 1852), 88.

This etching of a canal and lock system on the Erie Canal shows a boat entering the lower gate. The boat will then be raised to the water level behind the upper gate.

kinds of pretty. All the fellers are gonna be lined up askin' her to dance tonight, that's for sure," answered Ben.

"If she shows up, that is," offered Joe.

Just then, the doors to the building opened and a man came out and announced that it was time to come in for the dance. Cody walked in with the rest of the assembled crowd. He placed the apple pie on a table next to other items people had brought. He then selected one of the many wooden chairs that lined the outer walls of the large and open room and sat down to watch. People were still filing into the building two and three at a time. Their footsteps made loud clomping sounds on the hardwood floor and echoed around the room, and the floor made creaking sounds in some spots. The muffled sounds of a dozen different conversations began to fill the air. In one corner of the room,

Cody noticed three young men tuning their instruments: a guitar, a mandolin, and a fiddle.

Most of the early arrivals at the dance had been teenage boys and young men. Cody was beginning to wonder what kind of dance this was going to be when some of the first girls began to arrive. All the young men stopped their conversations and watched the parade of girls commence. The young women were all wearing what must have been their best and brightest formal dresses. Their locks were curled and pulled up high on their heads. It was a festive scene.

Cody noticed that, for the most part, the girls sat on one side of the room and the boys sat on the other. There were a few couples here and there that seemed to be steady boyfriend and girlfriend, but the singles weren't yet mingling. There were a lot of stolen glances across the room between groups of boys and girls, though. Groups of boys could be seen leaning into little circles and whispering. Groups of girls could be heard breaking out into demure little giggles. It was an atmosphere to which Cody could relate. Teenage dances hadn't really changed that much over all these years.

Then she arrived. All the heads in the room seemed to turn in unison to look at the new girl in town as she entered the room. Cody was smitten the moment he first looked at her. The girl looked to be about sixteen years old. She wore a dark blue dress and had sandy blonde hair. Her facial features were strikingly beautiful, set off by the most intensely piercing pair of hazel eyes Cody had ever seen. Within a moment after she arrived, both camps in the room were buzzing in little groups of conversation again. Cody could sense some envy coming from the groups of girls, and he knew for sure what the boys were saying—he was thinking the same things. Cody began to wonder whether he would be able to work up the nerve to talk to the new girl. He knew that if it were purely up to him, he would probably sit and be a wallflower, too shy to approach her. He had always been shy in situations like this. But perhaps David was more of the outgoing type.

Soon the room was pretty well filled to capacity. Cody guessed that there were forty or fifty people. Boys seemed to outnumber the girls, though, and it was clear that if any boy was going to catch the attention of a girl, he would have to be aggressive. Sure enough, as the musicians began to strike up the first tune, some boys sprang into action. Cody hesitated, then made a bold decision to follow suit. *Why not?* he thought. He made a beeline straight for the new girl. He felt a whirlwind of excitement and fear—this was not something he was used to doing.

Just before Cody reached the girl, he felt the familiar swimming sensation that always preceded his exit from a journal. When he opened his eyes, he was sitting back in his bedroom.

He felt a mixture of relief and regret at having left the journal at the moment he did. He was relieved a bit because he was pretty nearly terrified at approaching the pretty girl, having no idea what he was about to say, yet he couldn't help feeling excited to go back and find out. He had a feeling it wouldn't take long for him to go back into this journal.

15

Although he wasn't in the mood to waste time, Cody took a snack break. He felt the tingling sensations of the teenage crush, though he didn't even know the new girl's name yet! Still, he needed to know more about Metamora and the canal. Turning to his computer, he did an Internet search on the subject. He soon learned that the canal route ran from around Cambridge City in the northeast down to the Ohio River at Lawrenceburg in the southeast. It was built in stages because the state ran out of money in 1839, when the canal only stretched from Lawrenceburg to Brookville. The canal was extended a little at a time over the next few years, with the hope of tying the canal in with the whole Erie Canal system. The shallowness of the Whitewater River meant that most boat travel was prohibited, so the canal was an important alternative for cargo and passenger traffic. However, the growth of the railroad across the state in the 1840s and 1850s meant the canal was soon obsolete.

Learning that, Cody wondered just how long David and his father could have been in business as lock tenders. Maybe there was more in the journal. Gulping down his soda, he rushed back to his desk and found his place in the journal.

As I approached the girl, I found myself looking into the most stunning pair of eyes I had ever seen. I am normally not shy around girls, but I was struggling to find the words I needed to speak. I felt the sweat beginning to soak through my shirt. . . .

As he read these words, Cody again felt himself being transported through the dark spinning tunnel into the journal. When he opened his eyes, he was gazing into the eyes of the new girl. They were hazel with little flecks of light brown. They seemed to burn right through to Cody's brain, and he feared that it would turn him into a babbling idiot.

"M-m-my name is David Carter. I am very pleased to meet you," Cody said awkwardly, extending his right hand.

This map shows three main routes of the Underground Railroad in Indiana. The eastern route travels through Franklin County, near Metamora along the Whitewater Canal.

The girl did a slight curtsy and gently placed her hand in his. "My name is Emily Morris. I am pleased to make your acquaintance," she said.

Cody had always hated dancing, but he didn't have much choice here. Emily seemed to be waiting for him to do or say something. "Would you like to dance?" Cody asked.

"It would be my pleasure," answered Emily.

The pair took to the dance floor. The only type of dancing he had ever tried was a couple of slow dances at school, which were little more than a boy and a girl standing face to face at an awkwardly close distance with their hands around each others' waists, swaying slowly back and forth in one place. This, on the other hand, was real dancing, but Cody managed not to make too many mistakes as he led Emily around the floor.

"I am told your family just moved here from Pennsylvania," Cody said.

"That's right," answered Emily. "We come from around Pittsburgh."

"What brings you to Metamora?" he asked.

Emily paused awkwardly for a second before answering. "My father's work." She quickly changed the subject. "Where does your family live, and what do you do?"

Cody couldn't help but notice that his question had made Emily uncomfortable.

"We live a little ways out of town right along the canal. My dad's a lock tender there."

"That sounds interesting," said Emily. "Do a lot of passengers use the canal coming up from the Ohio River?"

Cody was glad he had done his research. "Yes, we get mostly small cargo boats, but there are always a few passengers that come through every day," he said. "My mother sells quite a few baked goods to the passengers when they stop at the lock."

Cody sensed that Emily had asked that question for a specific purpose, but she didn't follow up on it. He wondered why she had changed the subject so quickly when the topic of her father's work had come up.

"It's a little hot in here. I could use a glass of punch and some fresh air," Emily said.

Cody was relieved to stop dancing, and he took her hint. "Well, let's go get some refreshments."

The two headed for the table with the food and punch bowl. They each got a glass of punch and then headed outside.

"Could you show me the lock your father tends?" Emily asked. "I'd like to know more about it."

"Sure," Cody replied, a bit surprised. The pair began to walk the short distance to the Carter home.

They walked together in silence for a few moments before Emily spoke. "So tell me, where did your family come from before you landed here in Indiana?"

Again, Cody sensed that there was an ulterior motive behind this question. There was something about the way she was asking—it was as if Emily was feeling him out—searching for something. He couldn't be sure, but he got the distinct impression that he was being interviewed. He was glad he remembered the facts about the family that David had mentioned in the journal.

"We came from Kentucky," answered Cody, "but we moved up here in 1836 when work on the canal started. My pa got hired as a canal worker."

"So you're a southern boy, eh?" Emily said.

"I guess so, by birth anyhow," Cody answered.

"Did your family own slaves in Kentucky?" asked Emily.

Cody paused. He wasn't sure. He remembered that Edward Carter Sr. had mentioned that his father had owned slaves in North Carolina, but had David's family in Kentucky? He decided to play it safe. "Well, I don't remember much about living in Kentucky. I was just about six years old when we moved to Indiana."

"I have seen a lot of slaves," said Emily. "Runaway slaves, that is. A lot of them come through Pittsburgh on their way north. Some folks there help hide them on their way through."

Cody knew she was referring to the Underground Railroad, a network of people who worked together to help escaped slaves reach freedom in the north. He also knew not everyone agreed with its goals. "Yes, I have heard of that," he replied. "It has a lot of folks talking. Some say it's great what the abolitionists are doing, and some say they ought to be rounded up and thrown in jail."

"What do you say about it, David?" Emily asked.

Again, Cody hesitated. What would David have said? "I don't know what to think about it," he replied slowly. "I can see both sides. The southern farmers lose an awful lot of money when slaves run away. I can see why they wanted a fugitive slave law to force folks to help return their slaves, but then again, maybe slavery ought to be a thing of the past. I know if I was a slave who was on the run, I would sure appreciate the kindness of strangers to help me along my way."

There was a long pause. Then Emily spoke. "David, can you keep a secret?"

"Sure," replied Cody. He realized that he would have said yes to any request Emily made. How could anyone say no to her?

"I'm happy to hear you say that you understand why people would break the law to help slaves," Emily began. "David, when I told you earlier that my father's work brought us to Indiana, I didn't tell you what kind of work he did. I have to be very careful what I say because he is an abolitionist—and so am I. It's very important that this information remains a secret. Some who would hear it would immediately turn us in. But I liked you and trusted you from the minute you walked up to me at the dance. Something just told me that you could be trusted with my secret."

They walked along in silence again. Cody thought it was great news that Emily and her family were abolitionists and helped slaves on the Underground Railroad. He wanted to tell her that, but would David have agreed?

"Why did you decide to tell me about this?" Cody finally asked.

"Like I said, I like you and feel like I can trust you," Emily replied. "Also, to be totally honest, when you said you worked as a lock tender on the canal, it gave me an idea. You may not be willing to do this, but I need to ask you anyway. Your job here on the canal could be a great deal of help to our cause. When slaves run north and reach this side of the Ohio River, they cross into free land, but their trip is far from over. Bounty hunters wander the north side of the river throughout its entire length, constantly looking for any sign of runaway slaves and for any sign of those who would help them. That is why the Underground Railroad extends all the way to Canada: Fugitives aren't truly safe until they leave the country. This canal would be an excellent passage through this part of Indiana for escaping slaves. They could hide in cargo crates on canal boats. It would take some clever packaging, and it might also require willing lock tenders to look the other way when they came through, if you follow my meaning."

"You are asking me to help you run slaves through the canal?" Cody asked. "I'm not sure that's possible. What if someone finds out?"

"It isn't likely anyone would find out," said Emily. "Most of the people who help us in situations like this simply agree not to investigate any suspicious-looking cargo crates. They know there is a possibility that a slave could be hidden on the boat, but they don't bother to look into it. That's all there is to it, really. If a slave gets caught past your location, you would simply play dumb. No one would likely suspect you of being involved. That is the way the

Pleasant Home Ky
Sept 16

Dear Sister

your very kind letter of Sept the 1st has been recieved and I am greatly obliged to you for the solicitude you seem to manifest to sett me right as well as the taunt at which you presume to my ignorance You say since this war commenced you have read the constitution a great deal of late &c now I will not presume to be a constitutional critic nor does boast of any great knowledge of the law there are matters that seem better adapted to the consideration of states men and politicians than she who superintends the domestic office of a family But in states where abolitionism womans rights and free negroism are common topics of discussion by the ladies I am not surprised to recieve a lecture upon my ignorance or my christianity because a set of principles and doctrins so repugnant to the best interests of society as well as the interest and happiness of the people of our once happy country you may think it strange that I do not wish to put myself on a level with a negro or that I do not want a negro put on a level with me if I did I should certainly be in favor of free negroism I am of the opinion that the slave should ever remain where our tilting places them under the constitution more over this is a State Right as I understand it and the people of indianie have no more right to meddle with the slaves of Kentucky than the people of Ky have to interfere with the property of citizens of indiannia And the constitution of the united States recognises this this principle which has been acted on from the establishment of our government to the inauguration Mr Lincoln and the fugitive Slavelaw is but a contempis of the constitution requiring a slave in a free State to be returned to his master upon proof of his

This is the first page of a letter written ca. 1862 by Mary Elizabeth Clark of Henry County, Kentucky, to her sister, Emily Ross, of Howard County, Indiana. In the letter, Mary Elizabeth appears to respond to her sister's pro-abolition views by stating her own belief that slaves should not be equal to white citizens. She also states that the war is a states' rights issue, and the people of Indiana do not have the right to tell the people of Kentucky what they can do with their property.

system works. There isn't a lot of communication between the people who are a part of this, which makes it very difficult for the authorities to get to the bottom of things."

It made perfect sense to Cody, and he wanted to agree to it right away. Of course, he probably would have agreed to carry runaway slaves to Canada on his back for Emily if she had asked him. But he again wondered whether David would feel the same.

"I would like to help you, Emily, really I would," Cody said. "But I just don't know if I can. Let me think on it for a day or two and give you an answer later. Is that alright?"

"Of course. I know it is a big decision," Emily replied.

"And don't worry," Cody continued. "Your secret is safe with me, no matter what I decide to do."

"I trust you," said Emily, as she reached up and gave Cody a little kiss on the cheek.

With that, Cody again felt the swimming sensations in his head, calling him back out of the journal. When the curtain began to open before him, he was back in his room.

Cody reached up and gently touched the spot on his cheek where Emily's lips had just pressed. How could David Carter even consider turning down Emily's request?

16

Emily's request seemed like a no-brainer. How could any self-respecting, red-blooded American boy say no to such a lovely creature? But when he really stopped to think about it, Cody realized it wasn't as simple as he was making it. It was a different time. Most people, even those in the northern states who wanted to ban slavery, still hadn't come to the point where they saw the races as equal. Helping slaves escape was, no doubt, a very difficult decision for someone to make in 1846. Cody understood that he had to be careful when judging people of another time from the viewpoint of his own time. After all, if people from those times were to look at some aspects of twenty-first century society, they would have a pretty poor opinion of some of those morals, too. Cody decided he would just have to give David the benefit of the doubt and trust that he would make the decision that was best for him in the long run.

Cody didn't want to wait around to find out what that decision would be, so he went right back to the journal. The fact that he wanted to see Emily again played no small role in his decision. He found his place and began to read.

Emily's request weighed heavily on my mind that night. After she left, I went to bed and tossed and turned for much of the night, mulling over my options. I honestly don't know where I stand on the issue. I do not hate the abolitionist movement as some people I know do. In my own opinion, slavery has worn out its welcome. However, I also understand that many people in the south, including some of my own kin, no doubt, base their whole livelihood on their slaves. Their slaves are their wealth. What is to become of these people if their slaves are suddenly taken from them? I find myself feeling that perhaps this Underground Railroad is a good solution to the problem. Perhaps if enough slaves are able to find their freedom, a few at a time, it will help to begin the process of phasing out slavery altogether. I don't know the answer, but I do feel like I am finding my answer to Emily's request. . . .

Reading these words, Cody felt the familiar swimming sensations, and the dark spinning mineshaft carried him back to Metamora. When he opened his eyes, he was standing at the canal lock with Oliver Carter.

"Your ma tells me you operated the lock for a boat all by yourself yesterday," said Oliver. "How did it go?"

Cody remembered how he was able to guide the boat through the lock. "No problems at all," he replied.

"She also tells me that she saw you walkin' along the towpath with a girl last night after the dance," said Oliver with a little twinkle in his voice.

"That was Emily Morris," replied Cody. "Her family just moved here from Pennsylvania."

"Real pretty too, I'm told," teased Oliver.

Cody grinned. "I suppose you might say that," he admitted. He was silent for a moment. "What do you think about slavery?"

Oliver paused. "Well, I reckon I am ready to see it go," he said. "Course you know we have some slavery in our family down south. It has been a part of the culture down there for a right long time. I'm not goin' to stand in judgment of any man who chooses to own slaves, but I would just as soon see it done away with. I'm not ashamed to say it, although there are some folks who'd probably like to have me tarred and feathered if they heard me talk like this."

Cody was very glad to hear these words. He assumed this would make David's decision a little easier. He decided to confide in Oliver.

"If I tell you a secret, would you promise not to tell anyone or hold it against anyone?" Cody asked.

"Of course, son. You can tell me anything," said Oliver.

"Well, it's about Emily and her family," Cody began. "She told me something last night, and she asked me to do something for her, too."

Cody hesitated, unsure how to proceed.

"Go on, son, I'm listenin'," Oliver said. "Don't worry; your secret is safe with me."

Cody took a deep breath. "Emily and her family are abolitionists, and they help slaves escape on that Underground Railroad," he said. "They have come to Indiana to recruit people to develop a network of helpers. She asked me if I would be willing to help her allow slaves to pass through here hidden on canal boats. She said I wouldn't have to do anything except sort of look the other way and not poke around looking through crates. She said if any slaves got caught on up the line that they wouldn't trace it back to me."

"I see," said Oliver. "And what did you tell her?"

"I haven't told her anything yet," said Cody. "I told her I needed a day or two to think it over. What do you think? Do you think it's wrong?"

"It's against the law," said Oliver. "The law of *man*, that is, but I reckon God might see it differently. David, this is your decision. I'm not goin' to tell you what to do, one way or the other, but I will tell you this: If you choose to help Emily, I will be willing to help, too."

There it was, thought Cody. *This Oliver Carter is a fine man.*

"Thanks," said Cody. "I knew I could count on you. I'm going to tell Emily that we will help her."

With that, Cody was off to town to find Emily. He found her leaving the mercantile.

"Care to go for a little stroll?" Cody asked her.

"That would be lovely," replied Emily. She offered Cody her arm, and he led her back down the towpath beside the canal.

"I've been thinking about our talk last night," said Cody. "I even spoke to my father about it—don't worry; he can be trusted with our secret. He supports what you are doing, and so do I. We have agreed to do what we can to help you with your cause."

"I just knew that I could trust you, David," said Emily. "I could see it in your eyes. I spoke to my father about our talk, too. He has come up with a plan. He has been to some of the towns north of here on the canal and found some willing households to be stopovers for slaves. The runaway slaves will travel in large crates with false bottoms. When they reach the stops with safe houses, there will be people there to help them off the boats and into hiding in the houses. I will try to tell you the names of the boats that will carry fugitives so that you will be aware of the situation as much as possible. Remember—just act as if nothing is out of the ordinary and let them pass. The folks on up the canal will do the rest."

"Sounds fine," said Cody.

"I am so glad!" exclaimed Emily.

As Emily threw her arms around Cody, his head began to swim. When he opened his eyes, he found himself back in the present, somewhat disappointed. David had made the right decision, as far as Cody was concerned. But had David really had the chance to guide boats carrying escaped slaves? He quickly read on in the journal.

Then late one evening, just before dusk, I found myself alone at the lock. My parents were both in town. A cargo boat was heading north up the canal from the direction of Brookville. I began to make preparations to allow the boat to enter the lock chamber and to raise it to the next level of the canal. . . .

Cody opened his eyes, still a little shaky after being transported back into the journal. He studied the approaching vessel. There were no passengers except for the boat captain, and there were several boxes of freight on the deck. When the boat got near enough that Cody could hear the captain, he could tell that something was wrong.

"I have a problem," the captain called. "I am hoping I can count on you to help."

"What's the trouble, mister?" Cody asked.

"I am Captain Conrad Willis," the man answered. "I work closely with the Morris family, here in Metamora. I understand you know them pretty well."

Cody understood that the captain was tip-toeing around a delicate subject. He realized this must have something to do with smuggling a runaway slave. Suddenly, Cody began to feel very nervous.

"Yes, sir, I guess you could say that," Cody answered.

"We need to talk," said Captain Willis.

Once the boat was inside the lock chamber, Cody shut the gates behind it and opened the side-channel gates to start the process of allowing the chamber to fill with water. The boat slowly began to rise with the water level as the captain exited his boat and went into the little house with Cody.

"There is a bounty hunter following me," said Captain Willis. "I have a young male slave out there hidden in a box. The bounty hunter has a real good idea that the slave's in this boat. He was about an hour behind me. I got a warning by telegraph back in Brookville. He'll catch me for sure within an hour if I don't do something. I hate to even ask you this, but would you be willing to hide him here until the bounty hunter passes? I just don't know what else to do."

This can't be good, thought Cody. He felt himself begin to panic, though he knew David had agreed to help.

"There doesn't seem to be any choice, does there?" answered Cody.

"We just need to get him off here until the bounty hunter passes by," answered the captain. "Once the bounty hunter gets ahead of us, we'll be able to get the fugitive back on the move on another boat."

"Let's do it," Cody replied. "We'd better hurry."

The canal boat was about halfway up to the upper level of the canal. Cody followed the captain to the lock chamber. They stepped down onto the deck of the boat, and the captain walked over to a large wooden crate that reminded Cody of a tall coffin. He took a pry bar and opened the end of the box, which appeared at first glance to contain only some saddles. Then Cody watched as the captain tugged on the floorboard of the crate and it began to slide out. He pulled it all the way out and there, in a space that didn't look big enough, was a very frightened human being!

Cody could not believe his eyes. How could someone travel for hours on end in such a tight, dark place? There was a little bit of straw on the floor to soften the ride slightly, but it looked to do little to provide any real comfort. The young man who was riding there seemed to be about eighteen to twenty years old. His eyes were wide with fright.

"Don't worry, son," the captain said to the escapee. "You'll be safe here. We have to make a stop here for a little while to allow a bounty hunter to pass on by. This young man is going to take good care of you until another boat can pick you up and carry you on up the canal."

"Yes, sir," said the escaped slave. "I surely thank you both for your kindness."

The young man struggled to get to his feet, having stiffened from lying in one position for so long. Even though dusk was quickly falling and the light of the sun was not very bright, Cody noticed that the young man was squinting as if it were high noon, likely from having been confined in nearly total darkness. The runaway was wearing tattered gray pants. He had no shirt or shoes.

As he and the captain helped the runaway slave out of the boat and up on the towpath, Cody was horrified to notice an ugly, crisscrossed network of raised welts and scars across the young fugitive's back. The injuries were old, but they were a permanent testament to what this poor soul had been through. Cody quickly turned away. For a moment, he thought he might be sick.

By the time the captain and Cody had gotten the young man out of the boat and into the little lock-tender's house, it was nearly dark.

"I have to be going," said Captain Willis. "The bounty hunter will be here any time now, I expect. He will be looking to search my boat. He can search in it now all he wants. I am going on up to Metamora. You can tell him where he can find me, but he'll be disappointed when he does!"

"What should I do if he wants to search here?" Cody asked.

"Hide the boy as best you can, but I don't expect the bounty hunter will think to search here," the captain replied. "I don't think he would expect us to unload a fugitive so close to town."

Cody opened the upper gates of the lock, and the horses began pulling Captain Willis's boat on toward Metamora. "There will be another boat along later to pick him up," said the captain as the boat began to move out of the lock. "Thank you kindly for your help."

Cody went into the house and found the young fugitive standing exactly where they had left him.

"My name is David," Cody said. "What is your name?"

"I am called Gabriel," the runaway responded.

"We need to find a place to hide you for a while," Cody said. "I expect there will be a man coming through here soon looking for you. Don't worry; I don't think he will even look here, but just to be safe, we need to find you a place to lay low."

"Yes, sir," Gabriel replied, "And thank you, sir. You are most kind."

Cody looked around the small house. "The only place I can think of to hide you in this little house is under my bed," he said. "Why don't you crawl under there and stay hidden? I'll go out and watch for anyone coming to look for you."

Gabriel crawled into yet another tight space. It was a drill he seemed used to by now. Cody went outside and manned his post at the lock, hoping for the best. Within twenty minutes, Cody heard a horse coming up the towpath from the south. As the rider came nearer, Cody could see that the man rode with a purpose.

"Are you Oliver Carter, the lock tender?" the man asked.

"No, sir. I am David, his son," Cody answered.

"Have you seen any suspicious activities here on the canal of late?" asked the man. "My name is Charles Winthrop, and I am tracking down a fugitive slave. We have received some information that there might be some valuable cargo being smuggled through these parts—this cargo is private property that needs to be returned. It is my duty to try to bring that property back to the rightful owners, and under the Fugitive Slave Act, it is your duty to report anything you might know about it. Do you know anything about it?"

Cody felt a chill run up his spine. He had never been good in situations like this. He was not a good liar. He had the kind of face that tended to give him away. Luckily, it wasn't his real face that was staring down Mr. Winthrop.

"No, sir, I sure don't know anything about it," Cody replied, cool as a cucumber. "If I ever hear of anyone trying to sneak a fugitive by me, they won't get far. I come from the South, sir. I'll be sure to keep my eyes and ears open. Thanks for the information, Mr. Winthrop."

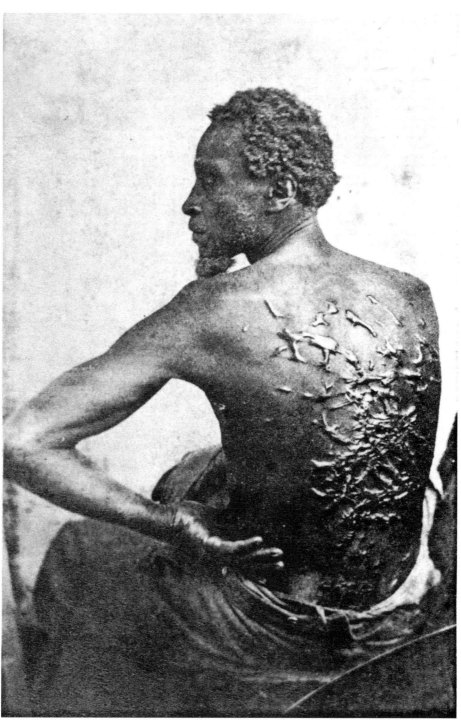

A former slave turned Union soldier during the Civil War reveals scars on his back from whippings. Gabriel would have had similar scars.

Winthrop took a long look at Cody, sizing him up. The performance seemed to satisfy him. "Thank you for your time. Be sure that you report anything suspicious," he said as he climbed back into his saddle.

"I will for sure," Cody replied. "Good night to you, and good luck."

Cody watched the man ride on into Metamora. He was sure that Winthrop would track down Captain Willis and demand to search his boat. He was not at all sure what would happen when he found the boat to be free of fugitive slaves.

Cody walked back into the house. He told Gabriel to stay hidden under the bed, just in case Winthrop decided to double back and check the lock house.

"Where do you come from, Gabriel?" Cody asked.

"Down 'round Tennessee—close to Memphis, sir," came Gabriel's reply from under the bed.

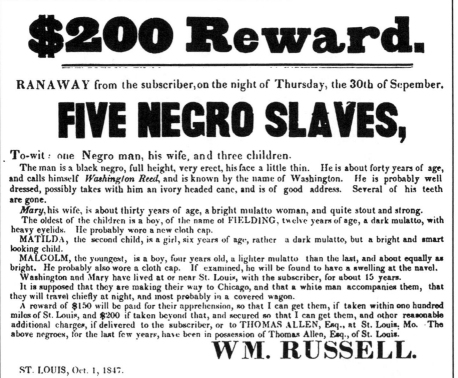

Newspapers regularly published notices seeking the return of runaway slaves. This notice, published in Missouri in 1847, states that a reward would be offered for the capture of a family believed to be on the run from Saint Louis, Missouri, to Chicago, Illinois.

"How old are you?" Cody inquired.

"Don't rightly know for sure," answered Gabriel. "My Massa told me I was born in 1827, but I don't know the date. My mammy was sold off when I was just little. I don't have no family much to help me keep track of how old I am."

"Well, if you were born in 1827, that would make you about nineteen years old," Cody offered.

"Nineteen," repeated Gabriel. "That don't seem like too long, but I feel like it's been a lot longer. Thank you again, sir, for your kindness."

"You can call me David," Cody replied.

Then Cody heard someone coming up the towpath toward the house. He quickly told Gabriel to be quiet, then walked outside. He breathed a little easier when he saw David's parents walking toward the house.

"There's a bounty hunter in town," said Oliver. "We were worried that he might have stopped here and given you a hard time."

"He stopped here," Cody replied. "But he didn't give me too hard a time. I was able to convince him I was on his side—good thing too, considering."

"Considering what?" asked Mary suspiciously.

"Considering I have what he's looking for under my bed right now!" Cody said.

"You mean you have a runaway in the house?" asked Oliver. "And with a bounty hunter here snoopin' around?"

"Yes, indeed," Cody said with a sly, proud smile. "Has the bounty hunter left?"

"He searched a boat and left in a hurry going on north," answered Mary. "Where's the runaway now?"

"His name is Gabriel, and he's still under my bed," Cody replied. "I guess it's safe to let him out from under there now."

The family entered the house. "Gabriel, my parents are here," Cody called out. "It's safe to come out from under there now. The bounty hunter has already gone."

"Yes, sir, Mr. David," said Gabriel as he crawled from under the bed.

"My goodness, look at you," said Mary. "You are half naked and dirty. You could probably use a good meal, too. David, he is close to your size. Get Gabriel some fresh clothes to wear, and I will warm him some of our supper leftovers."

In about an hour, Oliver Carter heard a boat coming up the canal from the direction of Brookville. He went outside to operate the lock. In a moment, he was shouting something to David.

"What do you need, Pa?" asked Cody as he stepped outside to investigate.

"This man is here to take Gabriel on up the canal," Oliver replied.

Cody reentered the house to find that Gabriel was ready. Gabriel emerged from the Carters' home in a clean set of clothes and with a belly full of home-cooked food. Before boarding the boat and entering yet another cramped hiding place, Gabriel paused to speak. "Miss Mary, Mr. Oliver, Mr. David, you good people will never know what your kindness has meant to me. I know that lots of other white folks would want to kill you for what you are doin' to help me. You make me feel like there are people left in this world that I can trust. I won't ever forget it."

"You just be careful and take care of yourself," said Mary.

"I hope you find a good life up north," Cody said. "You are due some good fortune."

The family watched as Gabriel crawled under the false bottom of a crate. The boat's captain covered him with the false floor and tacked the end of the crate closed with a hammer and nails. With that, Oliver opened the lock gates and the horses began to pull Gabriel north up the canal toward a tenuous freedom and an uncertain future.

The next morning Cody ran to Metamora to report what had happened to Emily. He found her sitting on the porch of her home.

"Emily, we have to talk," Cody said.

"I heard there was some excitement at the lock last night," Emily said.

"I had to hide a runaway slave under my bed!" Cody said in an excited tone. "His name was Gabriel. A bounty hunter came by looking for him. He was asking a lot of questions. He said there were reports that fugitives are being smuggled through here. I think I was able to convince him that I didn't know anything about it. I tried to make him think that I was on his side. I'm pretty sure he believed me, but I can't know for sure."

"It sounds like you handled it well," Emily assured him. "This sort of thing happens all the time. It isn't anything to get too worried about. Of course they know that slaves are being smuggled through the area. Slaves have been smuggled through all the possible routes out of the South for years. The hunters come through trying to scare folks into talking and telling what they know.

I think you handled it perfectly. There is no way he can trace anything to us. David, I am so proud of you!"

With that, Emily threw her arms around Cody's neck and gave him a long and passionate kiss. Cody thought his head would explode.

At that moment, he felt the swimming sensations again, pulling him from the journal. When the curtain began to open before him, he found himself sitting at his desk in his bedroom. He looked at David's journal and noticed there was one more short entry.

Jan. 21, 1847—asked for Emily's hand in marriage this evening. She said yes. We will be married in the spring!

"Way to go, David!" Cody exclaimed with pride.

PART SEVEN
The Journal of Andrew Carter
Corydon, Indiana, 1863

17

Cody had enjoyed his time in David Carter's journal. It was a welcome relief after the trauma of the Martin Carter journal. He hadn't had to worry about Indian attacks or battles. He had hung out with some teenagers and especially had enjoyed his time with Emily. He had also learned a lot about canals and how the Underground Railroad worked.

Now Cody looked into the box that contained the journals his grandfather had brought him. It was nearly empty. There was only one journal left. His timing was good, since on Monday, his family was leaving to visit his grandfather in Tennessee. He would have just enough time to finish reading, and then he would be able to share his experiences.

The next morning, after breakfast, Cody returned to his room and retrieved the last remaining journal from the box.

"Well, this is it," he said. "The last leg of my trip."

He opened the cover and read the title page. *The Journal of Andrew Carter, Corydon, Indiana—1863.* Cody knew Corydon was way down in the southern part of the state, near the Ohio River. He also remembered learning that Corydon was the original state capital of Indiana, before Indianapolis, but he was sure that had been way before 1863.

Eager to get started, Cody settled himself in, turned the page, and began to read the first entry.

My name is Andrew Carter. I am eighteen years old. I live in the town of Corydon, in Harrison County, Indiana. My mother is Nancy Carter. I never really knew my father, Thomas. He was killed in action during the war with Mexico when I was just a baby. We lived in Tennessee when my father was killed. After that, my mother decided to move us north into Indiana to be near some of her family. Her father and my grandfather, Wallace Nelson, lives here in Corydon. As I begin my journal, our nation is in a mess. The war between the states has been raging on for two years now. It doesn't show signs of stopping any time soon. I am torn between my love of country and my love of family. Much of my family still lives in states that have seceded from the Union—the secesh states. They are now under the government of the Confederacy. I am against the war, but I want to see the Union preserved. Some would call me a Copperhead for these views, but I don't know what to call myself. I am simply torn. . . .

Cody again felt the swimming in his head and a falling sensation. When he opened his eyes, he was standing in the center of a town. He was in a crowd of young people, two of whom seemed to be getting very worked up about something. As he continued to observe, he realized that they were arguing about the war. There seemed to be two camps in this debate. One group seemed to be very supportive of the Union army and President Lincoln. The other side seemed to be not so much against the Union as against the war itself.

"This war should never have been started in the first place," asserted one hot-tempered teenage boy with fiery red hair to match. "Lincoln stole the election! Most of my family is from the South. They depend on slave labor for their livelihood. Lincoln is trying to rob them of everything they have!"

"Nonsense, Jim," retorted a young man from the other group. "South Carolina and the other secesh states never gave Lincoln a chance. They started leaving before he even took office! He wasn't about to take their slaves away; he wanted to keep the Union together."

"That's what he says now, George," replied the red-haired teen, "but a lot of folks know better. He's an abolitionist at heart. He's said as much himself."

"He's also said that he would do whatever it took to preserve the Union, including keeping slavery in place," replied George.

"Well, whatever the case, it's way too late now," Jim replied. "We've got ourselves in a real, honest-to-goodness mess! I say we just end this war now and go back to the way things were before."

"The way things were before wasn't working, Jim," George answered. "Southern states kept trying to spread slavery further and further west into the new states and territories. Don't you see how that would bother the Northern states?"

"So you expect the South to just sit back and let all those new territories and states come in with slavery outlawed?" Jim asked. "You expect the South to let the North get a big advantage in power so that they can outvote us on

President Abraham Lincoln and his cabinet members examine a map at the beginning of the Civil War.

every issue in Congress? What's the matter with popular sovereignty? Why not let people vote to decide whether they want slavery or not? Majority rules, I say!"

"Yeah, sure," replied George sarcastically, "and if you don't have a majority, create one by shipping in people from all over to stack the vote for you. Look how that turned out in Kansas!"

There was a momentary pause, and tension filled the air. Suddenly, Cody decided to speak.

"You both make good arguments," he began. "I can see both sides of it. I truly can. I, too, have a lot of family in the South. I know how much slavery means to the whole Southern economy. I also know how important it is to pre-serve the Union. Can you just imagine how vulnerable we all are right now as we battle against our own brothers? What's to stop anyone around the world from coming in here and taking advantage of us in our time of weakness? What if the Confederate States of America succeeds in winning independence? How can we face the future as separate countries? One thing is for certain: both surviving countries would be far weaker than we are as one union. My heart tells me that we should, as Jim says, just end this and try to go back to the way things were before—but my head tells me that it's impossible to do that now. I fear there is no turning back. I fear we'll be forced to see this thing out to the bitter end."

Cody was impressed with himself. The little speech had made good sense. It seemed to strike a chord with the others gathered around him, too.

"Leave it to good old Andy Carter to be the voice of reason," said Jim.

"Yeah," agreed George. "We could argue until we're blue in the face, but we aren't going to change the reality of the situation. I think you hit the nail on the head, Andy."

As the group began to break up and head their separate ways, Cody thought about the scene he had just witnessed. He was a bit confused. Here he was in the free state of Indiana during the middle of the Civil War, and he had just witnessed a debate in which a lot of the crowd had strong Southern sympathies. How common was it for people in the North to feel this way?

As he considered the question, a middle-aged woman came out of the doorway of a small house down the road. "Andrew, where are you?" she called. "Supper's on the table gettin' cold."

Cody realized the woman must be Andrew's mother, Nancy Carter, and began to walk toward her. "Sorry," he called. "I got caught up in a little discussion in town."

"Debating this awful war again with Jim Watson and George Jenkins, no doubt," Nancy said, as Cody drew closer. "Those two are both stubborn as mules."

"Yeah," agreed Cody. "I believe they both think they're going to change the other one's mind if they keep talking long enough. Neither one really listens to the other."

"I bet you told them how you always see both sides. You always did have a level head, son," said Nancy. "I wish your father had been more like you in that way. He just up and volunteered to go fight in that Mexican war without so much as thinking it through once. He had to go off and get himself killed, and for what? So the United States could have a bunch of land that has done nothing but cause all of this fussing ever since. If it weren't for all that God-forsaken land your father died to gain, we wouldn't be in this war now!"

It was easy for Cody to see that Nancy Carter harbored a lot of bitterness about her husband's death. She seemed to see the Mexican War as a big cause of the Civil War, and from what Cody knew of it from history class, he could see her point.

TRICKS *v.* HONOURS.

South :—"OH! DON'T GIVE UP, ABE; TRY ANOTHER TRICK. I DON'T MIND. I HOLD ALL THE HONOURS."

This 1863 political cartoon depicts Lincoln cowering next to a Confederate soldier who wears patches with the names of battles that the South had won. The soldier tells Lincoln to try another trick because he holds all the honors. Lincoln was unpopular, even in the North.

"They say the United States gained a lot from that war," Cody said. "Maybe he didn't die in vain."

"I just don't see why men attach so much glory to war," responded Nancy. "I just don't see it. A man's life is about all he has when it comes down to it. He only gets to live in this world once. Why would a man be willing to throw it all away to gain land for his government? To my way of thinking, there are only two things worth fighting for: God and family."

"I know that some folks think that is exactly what this war is about—God and family," answered Cody.

Nancy sighed. "All I know is, I'm sure glad you haven't got mixed up in this fighting. I couldn't bear to lose you, too," she said softly.

Cody could see how upset she was by the idea of her son meeting the same fate as her husband. After a moment, he replied, "Well, I'm not even sure what side to support. I'm sure not planning to go and seek out a fight, but if I feel like I need to protect what we have here, I'm not likely to back away from anyone."

As he entered the house and walked toward the food spread out on the table, Cody felt himself being pulled out of the journal. Just as things began to go dark, he was back in his bedroom.

18

Cody had been fascinated by Jim and George's debate over the expansion of slavery. He had only recently studied this era in history class, and it was clear to him now just how polarizing the issue of the spread of slavery into western states and territories had been to the United States. He had known that on some level, of course, but he never knew just how difficult it was for ordinary citizens to decide where they stood on the issues that divided the country. It had always seemed obvious before, from the perspective of his own time: Slavery was wrong and needed to be ended. Yet, having just come from Andrew Carter's journal, Cody seemed to have more questions than answers. Perhaps what his history teacher had said was true: Maybe we do get a better look at history the further away we get from it.

Cody was ready to go back into this journal again. He found his place and began to read the next entry.

> *June 29, 1863—Things do not go well. Rumors are flying around like flies. Word is spreading that Confederate General John Hunt Morgan is on the move through Kentucky and plans on invading Indiana. They say he wants to bring the horror of war to the people of the North. Jim Watson claims he was approached by one of General Morgan's advance scouts yesterday. He says Morgan is looking for Southern sympathizers who might be willing to join his forces when he comes through. Jim is a lot of talk, but if what he says is true, we could be in trouble here in Corydon. . . .*

As he read these words, Cody felt the familiar sensations drawing him into the journal. When he opened his eyes, he once again was standing in a small crowd of young men. An older man in a Union military uniform was speaking.

"Good afternoon, men," the man said. "My name is Colonel Lewis Jordan. I command the Sixth Regiment of the Indiana Legion. You might know us as the Harrison County Home Guard. I am here on behalf of the governor of Indiana, the honorable Oliver Morton. We are trying to muster as many volunteers as we can to help stand guard for our communities here in the area. As you have probably heard, Rebel forces may be planning a raid. There are many conflicting reports as to where this might occur and how large the forces are. We have intercepted several telegraph messages, but the information is inconsistent. We believe this to be intentional, that the Confederates are planting the information in an attempt to confuse us. At any rate, we are in the process of preparing for any eventuality. Those who are willing are being asked to sign up and join the Home Guard. There is a real chance that if the Rebels cross the Ohio River into Indiana, they could come right through Corydon. Who will protect our town, men?"

General John Hunt Morgan (1825–1864) began his military career in the Mexican War and enlisted in the Confederate Army on October 27, 1861. Beginning in July 1863, Morgan led a band of Confederate soldiers on a raid through southern Indiana and Ohio.

CIVIL WAR MATERIALS, DC008, INDIANA HISTORICAL SOCIETY

Many of the young men assembled began to press forward to volunteer, but Cody hesitated. Would Andrew have volunteered?

"You going to sign up, Andy?" asked George Jenkins as he got into the line.

"Maybe," Cody replied. He remembered how upset Nancy Carter had been when speaking to Andrew about the war. "My mother would be devastated if I signed up to be in the militia. Ever since my pa was killed, her worst fear is to see me in uniform."

"You're old enough to make your own decision, Andy," George replied. "Do you really think your ma would want you to turn your back on this fight? These Rebels are liable to destroy this town. We have to be ready to stop them."

There was a long pause. George stood waiting for a reply. Cody looked down at the ground, deep in thought. He remembered Nancy's words: the only things worth fighting for were God and family. Wouldn't an attack on his community be an attack on family? Cody thought Andrew would believe so. He slowly stood up straight and looked George in the eyes, repeating Nancy Carter's words.

"My mother told me there were only two things she could see that were worth fighting for—God and family. If the Rebels try to march through our town and terrorize us, that's close enough for me. I'm going to sign up."

Once he had completed the enlistment process, Cody headed back for the Carter house. He wondered what he would tell Nancy and how she would react. When he got inside the house, though, he didn't have to say a word.

"You signed up for the Home Guard, didn't you?" Nancy asked.

"How did you know?" Cody answered.

"I am neither deaf nor blind. I see and hear things," she replied. "I saw Lewis Jordan ride into town about an hour ago. I knew why he was here."

"Are you disappointed in me for signing up?" Cody asked.

"Heavens no, dear," replied Nancy. "I'm proud of you. I'm disappointed that there is a need for you to sign up, but protecting your friends and family is as honorable a reason for fighting as I can think of. I just pray to God that you don't have to fire a shot and that you will be safe."

Cody thought of how his own mother might react if he enlisted in the military during wartime. He wrapped his arms around Nancy and gave her a tender hug. "I will be careful. I promise you that," he said.

Soon the men who had signed up to join the local militia met for training. They were put through their paces and drills. It was hot, and the drilling was hard, tedious work. They learned basic marching, starting over each time any-one of them would make a misstep. It all seemed a bit pointless to Cody, but they spent hours learning it until they became somewhat competent.

A more enjoyable aspect of the training, for Cody, was rifle drill time. Most of the men had plenty of experience shooting rifles, having spent plenty of time hunting from the time they were young boys. Military rifle training was a different matter altogether from hunting, however. First was the bayonet drill-ing. Cody had read about bayonets in books, but he had never seen them used in real life. The men had to learn how to affix the weapon to the end of their rifles. Then they practiced close combat by charging at large dummies hang-ing from post frames. They were instructed to jab the bayonet quickly into the dummy's midsection, then give an upward, twisting thrust before withdrawing the weapon. They practiced this over and over.

This map shows the route taken by General John Hunt Morgan's raiders. Traveling through Tennessee and Kentucky, they entered the southeastern part of Indiana, looting towns, taking weapons, and burning bridges. They pillaged several towns in Indiana and Ohio.

Shooting drills also were not what Cody expected. Most of the men could hit the targets easily and seemed impressed with themselves, but they quickly learned that hitting the target was only a small part of shooting in the military. They were drilled to shoot and then to reload as quickly as possible. They were told that a good soldier must be able to get off at least three shots in the space of a minute. This proved to be most difficult for the men to do, especially with drill sergeants screaming orders into their ears and firing their revolvers into the air to create an atmosphere of stress and tension. Eventually, most of the men became more proficient at reloading, although they remained far from the level of skill the drill sergeants expected.

Before long there were more than four hundred new volunteers under the command of Colonel Jordan. They were more a rag-tag assembly of farmers who could shoot than a well-oiled military machine. Cody was pleased with his own progress, though he remained anxious. What lay ahead for him, and Andrew? No sooner had the thought crossed his mind than his head began to swim, and he found himself back in his bedroom.

Cody's anxiety sent him immediately to his computer. Had Colonel Jordan been right about the threat to Corydon? Cody learned that an attack from General Morgan had been imminent, indeed. By July 8, Morgan's 1,800 men had reached the Ohio River. Although Morgan had been under orders from his superiors not to cross the Ohio River, he seemed bent on doing it all the same. His goal of hitting the North where they lived was important to him. With all the fighting taking place on Southern soil, Morgan felt that it was his personal project to bring a taste of the terror of war to the people of the North. Indiana braced itself for a bitter spoonful of that medicine.

Morgan's men seized two steamboats on the Ohio River, the *John B. McCombs* and the *Alice Dean*. He used these boats to transport his men across the river—the imaginary Mason-Dixon Line. The Confederate army set foot on Northern soil just east of the little town of Mauckport, Indiana. A small company of Indiana Home Guard was waiting there to attempt to turn the raiders back, but it was a woefully futile effort. Not only did Morgan's men chase off the Indiana guard, they confiscated a large part of their weapons in the process.

Once Morgan's men were on Indiana soil, they burned the *Alice Dean* and sent the *John B. McCombs* downriver. Morgan's men then marched north, away from the river—and toward Corydon and Andrew Carter.

19

What he had just learned made Cody nervous as he looked at the journal of Andrew Carter lying on the desk in front of him. Was he about to be a part of a Civil War battle? He couldn't recall learning about any fighting in Indiana. *Maybe this ends without a battle*, he thought hopefully. At any rate, he had come too far to turn back now. He quickly found the next entry and began to read.

July 9, 1863—An attack on Corydon is looking more and more certain. General Morgan's army advanced past the Home Guard stationed along their river-crossing route yesterday with no real difficulty. Word came to us that he is headed north, straight toward our position. We have been hard at work felling trees. We are using the logs to set up barricades about a mile south of town. We hope to use these as protection as we attempt to turn back the Rebels. . . .

As he read these words, Cody once again felt the sensations of being sent back into the past. When he opened his eyes, he found himself crouched behind a small pile of logs. At his side were George Jenkins and four other men whom he did not recognize. He looked around and saw many other such piles of logs with other groups of men huddled behind them. A militia captain was walking from log pile to log pile shouting orders and encouragement. He was heading toward Cody's group.

"Steady, men," the captain said. "Our scouts tell us that Morgan's men are less than a half mile away. Remember: work together, save your shots, and make each one count. We will be outnumbered. Don't forget our goal. We don't need to defeat Morgan; we just need to frustrate him and make him change his path. We are here to protect Corydon."

If the captain's words were meant to reassure, they fell short of the mark as far as Cody was concerned. He was in a near panic. There was an army of nearly two thousand experienced soldiers just a couple thousand feet down the road and coming right at them. *This is madness*, Cody thought.

THE CORYDON DEMOCRAT.

SIMEON K. WOLFE, Editor

CORYDON, IND., JULY 14, 1863

The Morgan Raid Into Indiana.

The Battle at Corydon.

450 Home Guards and Citizens.
vs:
4,500 Rebel Cavalry and 7 Pieces of Artillery.

The Home Guards & Citizens hold the Rebels in Check 25 Minutes.

Home Guards and Citizens Overpowered by Numbers and Compelled to Surrender.

CORYDON CAPTURED

Union Losses four Killed and two Wounded.

REBEL LOSS 10 KILLED AND 40 WOUNDED.

GREAT ROBBERY OF THE PEOPLE IN TOWN AND COUNTRY.

Our town and community have been the scene of intense excitement during the whole of the past week in consequence of the invasion of the State at this point by the notorious guerrillas under the equally notorious John Morgan. A vast amount of damage by horse-stealing and other plundering has been done which it is impossible for us to detail at the present time with any great degree of accuracy, but we think it a safe estimate to put the loss to our citizens at the least at $100,000.

We will endeavor to give a reliable account of the raid from the time the rebels crossed at Brandenburg up to the time when they left Harrison county. But for the lack of due military organization and the consequent official information on many points, our details may not be in every particular correct, but the main features we *know* are correct, for we were present in the midst of some of the exciting scenes and have a very lively recollection of them; of the other matters we think we have reliable accounts.

"Let's try to work together and coordinate our efforts," Cody heard George say. "We need to take turns shooting so that while we reload, we will have each other to provide cover fire. If we all fire at the same time, it will be too easy for Rebs to charge us while we are reloading."

Cody was impressed with George. He seemed to be a level-headed, reasonable young man. He had appreciated what George had to say in the debate with Jim Watson, and he was equally impressed with the apparent calm under pressure George was displaying now. It was sound advice, but Cody wondered just how well it would be carried out if the bullets started flying.

Cody didn't have to wonder long. Within a few short minutes, a shot rang out from a log barricade up near the front. Soon shots were coming from everywhere. One of the men Cody didn't know stood up to look over the log pile. He yelled something about Rebs and fired his rifle wildly in the direction of the oncoming soldiers. *So much for remaining calm under fire,* Cody thought.

On July 14, 1863, the front page of the Corydon Weekly Democrat *reported the news of Morgan's Raid into Indiana and the Battle of Corydon, where the Home Guard fought the raiders until Colonel Lewis Jordan raised the white flag of surrender. The casualties sustained were reported at four killed and two wounded for the Corydon Home Guard, while the Confederates sustained ten fatalities and forty wounded.*

Cody's senses soon were overwhelmed by the sights, sounds, and smells of real battle. Though he had learned a lot in school about historic battles, nothing could have prepared him for this experience. It was becoming difficult to see as the air grew thick with grayish-white smoke. Even worse, it was becoming hard to breathe. A dense smell of burning gunpowder hung everywhere, choking the young Hoosiers who were completely new to warfare. Cody's sense of hearing was also hard-hit. The nearly constant explosions of gunfire left a nerve-racking pounding in Cody's ears. Every few seconds, he could hear strange whistling and whirring sounds flying above him. He couldn't figure out what those sounds were at first. Then it dawned on him with horrific clarity—they were bullets flying over his head, some of them *just* over his head! The bullets made other frightening noises, as well. Sometimes they made a dull thud accompanied by a small explosion of dirt and dust as they pounded into the earth. Other times, they made a loud crack as they slammed into one of the protective logs behind which the Home Guard crouched, or there would be an echoing *piinngg* sound when a bullet glanced off a rock.

All these sounds rose in a cacophony of horror, yet there was a still more disturbing sound—one Cody *knew* he would never forget. It was the occasional sound of bullets slamming into flesh and bone and the accompanying screams of men in unimaginable pain and agony. Each time Cody heard it, he wanted to crawl under the log pile and curl up and hide.

The group of men with Cody did their best to work together, and none of them had been hit yet. Cody had fired his rifle twice, but he couldn't really see well enough to know if he had hit his target, or even come close. The battle seemed to last forever, but Cody had no idea how much time had really passed.

Cody saw some of the Home Guard troops start to flee back towards Corydon. Things seemed very bad. Before long, the order to surrender came down the line. The announcement was bittersweet for Cody. He felt defeated and demoralized, but the relative peace and quiet brought by the end of the fighting was more than welcome.

The Home Guard forces were gathered up, and their weapons were confiscated. Cody was very nervous.

"What will become of us?" Cody sheepishly asked George, who was standing in line next to him.

"I don't rightly know," George replied. "I reckon we're prisoners of war now. They'll probably either send us south to some prison, or maybe, if we're lucky, they'll ransom us and free us."

Cody wasn't sure exactly what George had meant, but he was relieved, at least, that he hadn't mentioned anything about a firing squad. After all the uninjured Home Guard were lined up and counted, they were ordered to march toward Corydon.

The march was short. Once in Corydon, the men were rounded up and kept in the yard of the courthouse. Cody watched in horror as the county commissioner walked outside the building with a rifle in his hand, a terrible mistake. A shot came from somewhere in the Rebel ranks, and the commissioner clutched at his chest. He attempted to speak, but only a pitiful gurgling noise came out as he fell to the ground and died.

The Home Guard prisoners seemed to be in shock, but Morgan's men were ready to make merry. The Rebel soldiers helped themselves to anything they wanted in the shops. They ransacked the town and stole money and any goods that struck their fancy. They even threatened to burn down the courthouse if they weren't given $1,000 from the county coffers. Cody was getting a better understanding of what George had meant by ransom.

To the Home Guard's great relief, Morgan paroled all of the prisoners. The Rebels had gotten their ransom at the expense of the town of Corydon. All the men had to do to earn their freedom was to promise not to take up arms against the South again, which, of course, all the men did, whether they meant it or not.

In the aftermath of the Battle of Corydon, Colonel Jordan gathered his remaining beaten-down troops and tried to encourage them.

"Keep your chins up, boys," the colonel said. "You have nothing to be ashamed of. You fought fiercely and admirably. We knew going in that it would be a nearly insurmountable challenge. We did all we could to throw those Rebs off course, and we gave them all they could handle. In fact, men, if war was strictly a numbers game, you would have made a fine showing. Reports are that Morgan lost ten soldiers, and forty more were wounded. They may be leaving us claiming a victory, but they're licking a lot of wounds. They know they have been in a scrap, that's for sure! We'll be better prepared for them if we ever have to face them again."

As the colonel's speech ended, everything started to go black and Cody's head started to swim. When he opened his eyes, he was back in his bedroom.

Cody had to know what happened next. He turned back to his computer and learned that after leaving Corydon, Morgan's Raiders had continued their march, heading northeast toward the Indiana towns of Vienna, Lexington,

This 1863 illustration shows Morgan's Raiders ransacking the town of Salem, Indiana, after the Battle of Corydon.

Vernon, Dupont, New Pekin, Salem, and Versailles, en route to their ultimate destination of Ohio. News about the attack on Corydon had spread quickly across the state. Since Corydon had been the original capital of Indiana, Hoosiers had felt this attack deeply. Governor Morton had called for help to track down General Morgan's Raiders and avenge Corydon. The battle led to a huge upswing in the number of Hoosiers who joined in service of the Union. Cody also learned that Morgan's Raiders were later overtaken and captured in Ohio.

Cody reluctantly closed the journal's cover. "I did it!" he exclaimed. "I made it through all the journals."

Andrew Carter's journal had been tough for Cody. He knew he would never forget the horrible sights, smells, and especially the sounds of battle. He had learned enough about war to know that he never wanted to see it again. He had a new appreciation for what soldiers went through to defend American freedom, and he hoped he would not take that for granted anymore.

As Cody sat, he reflected on all his experiences in the Carter journals. What a wild ride he had been on! He had killed his first buck, heard stories of meeting Blackbeard, and been through the emotional wringer of family tragedy in the Tuscarora Wars. He had made maple syrup with Daniel and Rebecca Boone, then hunted and traveled through the Blue Ridge Mountains with Daniel. He had witnessed treaty councils with Native Americans and experienced attacks on the mountain frontier. He had lived in a state that no longer existed. He found himself choking back emotion as he recalled losing his friend, Sitting Fox, at the Battle of Tippecanoe, and he felt pride in helping Gabriel, the runaway slave at Metamora. Then, to top it all off, he had just experienced the Battle of Corydon!

It was hard for Cody to wrap his mind around all of that, but then he was pestered by a thought. Everything he had experienced in the journal seemed like epic adventure. Now it was his turn to begin keeping a journal of his own.

"What in the world will I write about?" Cody said out loud. "Nothing exciting like this ever happens to me."

The thought began to eat away at him. Then he remembered he was heading to Tennessee on Monday. *Maybe Grandpa will have some ideas about this*, he thought.

Conclusion

Monday morning came early. Cody was still groggy as his family loaded up the car and headed for his grandfather's farm in Tennessee. The six-and-a-half-hour drive that lay ahead of them always seemed long to Cody. He was able to sleep for the first couple of hours, waking up as the family entered Kentucky. There was always something about crossing the Ohio River that got Cody excited. He loved looking out over the beautiful landscape of Kentucky as they headed south. The rolling hills began to turn to low wooded ridges as they got closer to Tennessee. By the time they left Interstate 75 and headed southeast on Highway 25E, the hills turned into mountains. They rolled on through the little town of Pineville, which was positioned in a valley below towering wooded ridges. They were in Daniel Boone country now, Cody realized. Soon they would reach the town of Middlesboro and enter the Cumberland Gap tunnel.

They entered the mile-long tunnel in Kentucky and emerged in Tennessee. It was directly below the very route Boone had carved out and used to lead settlers into Richard Henderson's Transylvania Colony.

Cody was excited to see his grandpa again. He looked forward to the blue-and-white sign that welcomed people into Tennessee, as he always got the feeling that he was being welcomed home. After another hour and a half of winding through one valley after another, Grandpa's farm came into view.

Cody's grandfather was waiting in the living room to welcome them. Cody greeted him with a big hug.

"How are those journals comin' along?" Grandpa asked.

"I just finished them this weekend," Cody answered. "I want to talk to you about them. I have a few questions to ask."

"I just figured you might," said Grandpa with a knowing wink. "We'll sit 'n talk after supper."

Later, Cody stuffed himself on good country cooking, and then he and his grandfather went out to the front porch. Cody drank in the beautiful view of the valley as he sat down in a chair.

"How was your trip?" asked Grandpa.

"Oh, pretty good," answered Cody. "Traffic wasn't too bad, so we made pretty good time."

"I ain't talkin' about your trip today," Grandpa interrupted. "I mean the journals."

Cody suddenly felt strangely shy. He hadn't anticipated it, but it was sort of hard to share what he had been through with his grandfather. The experience of traveling through the journals now seemed to be an intensely personal thing, even though he knew his grandfather had gone through it, too.

"Why didn't you tell me what happens when we read the journals?" Cody asked. He didn't like asking that question. It came out sounding accusatory, but Cody couldn't stop it.

"It's just somethin' that we all go through alone. It's a sort of rite of passage, I guess you could call it," Grandpa replied. "Not knowin' ahead of time is just part of the process. Every Carter has to find his own way through it the best he can."

"You mean like a *pa-waw-ka*, right?" Cody said.

"I believe you got a lot out of those journals after all," Grandpa replied with a knowing smile.

For the next hour, Cody and his grandpa discussed the details in the journals. They each shared their own feelings about what they had felt and experienced in the stories. Then Cody decided to ask the question that had been bothering him about writing his own journal.

"There is just one thing I have been wondering about all this, Grandpa," said Cody.

"What's that?" asked Grandpa.

"Well," continued Cody, "it's just that I don't know how I am going to be able to write a journal of my own. How does my life stack up with all the history that is in those journals? Who's going to want to read about my life? It's kind of boring when you compare it to what I just read."

"I understand what you're sayin', Cody," said Grandpa. "There is somethin' you don't know about the journals, though. You see, I didn't give you all the journals. I just picked out the ones I knew you'd like. There are a lot more, but not all of them are as excitin' as the ones you've read. My journal's among the one's you haven't read yet. I figure you'll want to wait until I am gone before you read that one. That's usually the way it works. It wouldn't do to read a journal of someone who is still livin'."

"I can understand that," Cody responded, "but what about the journals that aren't that exciting? What if my journal turns out to be boring?"

"That's the thing about history, Cody," Grandpa answered. "Everybody always thinks it is somethin' that happened to other people a long time ago. The fact is, history is happenin' right now. We're all a part of it. Sometimes, our experiences happen at just the right time and place to make for an interesting story that goes into the history books, but most of the time, our experiences are more ordinary. It doesn't make our lives boring or unimportant; that's just the way it is. I figure if history is happenin' to us, we might as well go ahead and write it down, just in case it gets excitin'. If you watch what's goin' on close enough and write it all down, somebody down the line will want to read about it—that's just the way it goes. You don't think ol' Ethan Carter thought that makin' all that maple syrup with Daniel and Rebecca Boone was excitin' or that people would one day want to read about that, do you?"

Then Cody understood. It was like his history teacher said: Sometimes we do get a better view of history the further we get away from it. Sometimes, when you're living through something, you don't see it as history. It's just life—but life *is* history, and history *is* life. And that, Cody thought, might be a good first entry in his own journal.

Afterword
What Was Fiction and What Was Real?

For me, the fun thing about writing historical fiction is that I get to take history and add my own flavors and spices to it. The overall historical back-story that runs throughout this book is based in fact.

Going into the writing process, I knew that I wanted to write about some parts of history that don't get a lot of coverage in textbooks—such as the state of Franklin. I also had settings in mind. I wanted to start in coastal North Carolina. My family vacations in the Outer Banks each summer, near Beaufort, where the first journal takes place. From there, I gradually wanted to move westward and northward with the time line. I wanted to set some chapters in eastern Tennessee in the area that was once the state of Franklin. My grand-father really does have a farm in Hawkins County, Tennessee, in what was once part of Franklin, and my father was born and raised there. I also knew that I wanted the book to end up in Indiana, my home state. So, I planned Cody's family history to follow a path similar to my own. Writing coaches always say to "write what you know," and that is what I have tried to do in this book.

As far as what is real and what is fiction, I will attempt to break that down journal by journal.

Part One—Journal of Edward Carter

The story of Edward Carter and his family is fictional. The setting is real. The description of Beaufort is accurate; Beaufort is a beautiful little seaport town and the fourth oldest town in North Carolina.

Blackbeard really did run aground off the coast of Beaufort, and he really did meet his end on Ocracoke Island, several miles north, up the coast from Beaufort. The story of Blackbeard meeting the two Edward Carters was just a flight of fancy on my part, though Blackbeard really did come into the town of Beaufort after his ship was stranded.

The Tuscarora Wars did happen as described. The attack on Edward Carter's grandparents, while fictional, is based on many similar real-life events.

Part Two—Journal of Ethan Carter

The setting of this journal is based on real events. Daniel Boone did live in the Yadkin Valley during this part of his life. Ethan Carter is fictional, so his relationship with the Boones is just a fun story I used to introduce Daniel Boone. Boone is a fascinating character who I think does not get enough mention in most textbooks. I've read a lot of books that tell his amazing story, and I hoped to stir up an interest in him through these chapters. I encourage readers to read more about him and others like him—Simon Kenton, for instance, whose exploits read like superhero adventures.

The places that Boone and Ethan travel on their hunting trip are real. Pilot Mountain and Blowing Rock are actual North Carolina landmarks. The story of how Blowing Rock was named is my interpretation of the Native American myth. The wind really does blow straight up this cliff and often returns lightweight items to people who throw them over the edge. It is known to rain and snow straight upward there.

The accounts of Daniel Boone's service during the French and Indian War at the Battle of the Wilderness are true. Also, we really do call dollars *bucks* because that was the monetary value of one deerskin on the frontier.

Part Three—Journal of Landon Carter

In parts three and four, the line between fiction and reality becomes more blurry. Landon Carter, who is a prominent figure in both his own journal and in Annabelle Carter's, is loosely based on a real person. In researching the state of Franklin, I noticed that the speaker of the Senate's name was Landon Carter. I saw that his father, John Carter, had been a prominent leader at Fort Watauga years earlier. It was just through dumb luck on my part that I uncovered prominent Carters in researching this part of the book, so I went with it. Although their names and positions are real, their actions and words in this book are fictional.

The story of the Treaty of Sycamore Shoals and Richard Henderson's failed Transylvania Colony is real. The people mentioned as being in attendance, Native American and white, were really there. The speech given by Dragging Canoe is real, though slightly paraphrased. The rest of the conversations that took place come strictly from me.

The stories of the Indian attacks on Fort Watauga and other area forts are real. Dragging Canoe's cousin, the Cherokee Beloved Woman, Nancy Ward, did warn the settlers of the attacks. John Sevier did save Bonnie Kate Sherrill and help her over the wall of the fort. Sevier was married to another woman when that happened, but after his first wife later died, he and Bonnie Kate were married.

Again, as is the case throughout the book, all the conversations contained within the real events come from my own mind, based on the characters and my research.

Part Four—Journal of Annabelle Carter

Landon Carter plays a major role in this journal as well, this time as an adult. Again, he is loosely based on the real Landon Carter. Annabelle Carter is fictional. I thought it would be fun to have one of the journals be written by a girl. I hoped it might open the door for a little comic relief for Cody to have to experience life in the person of a girl.

The story of the Battle of King's Mountain at the beginning of Chapter 9 is true. The story of the state of Franklin is true.

The gathering of the settlers into Fort Watauga for safety from possible attack is fictional in this instance, but is based on many such incidents that happened on a regular basis in that time period.

Part Five—Journal of Martin Carter

Martin Carter is fictional. The setting around Vincennes in the Indiana Territory is true. Of course, Governor William Henry Harrison is real and his home is called Grouseland. The description of the relationship and tension between Harrison, Tecumseh, and the Prophet is true, although somewhat simplified.

Sitting Fox is fictional. I wanted Martin to have a Native American friend. I wanted this relationship and its tragic ending to be the reason Cody's father, Mark, was not able to handle his own attempt at the Carter journal experience.

The story of Sitting Fox's *pa-waw-ka*, while fictional in his case, is a real tradition among the Shawnee. The story of Sitting Fox's *pa-waw-ka* is based on the true story of the young Tecumseh earning his. I have read the account of Tecumseh's *pa-waw-ka* experience in multiple books, and it is very similar to what Sitting Fox went through in this book.

The Battle of Tippecanoe actually did happen. It helped propel Harrison to the presidency years later when he and his running mate, John Tyler, used the campaign slogan, "Tippecanoe and Tyler Too." That battle did not end the trouble with Tecumseh, who later joined forces with the British to fight against the Americans in the War of 1812. Tecumseh was killed during this war in 1813 while fighting in the Battle of the Thames in Canada.

Part Six—Journal of David Carter

I used David Carter's fictional family to tell two stories. I wanted to write a bit about the importance of canals in the years just before the railroads became prominent in Indiana. I also wanted to bring in Indiana's role as a key part of the Underground Railroad. I decided to set this journal in Metamora, Indiana, because of its central location on the canal and because I know it well, as it is near my hunting grounds.

The Whitewater Canal still flows through the town of Metamora and the vicinity. There was a lock at the same location as described in the book. In fact, the lock is still there, about one mile south of Metamora on US Highway 52.

I used the fictional Emily and the Morris family as a way to bring in a love interest and introduce an abolitionist family. The secretive nature of such families and their forbidden work was told in as accurate a way as I could manage. Runaway slaves occasionally were transported on canal boats. Gabriel's travels on the canal are my own interpretation of how this may have been done.

Part Seven—Journal of Andrew Carter

This journal was a pleasant surprise for me. My original outline for the book had this journal set in Indianapolis during the Civil War, but my research took me to another place. I learned that Corydon, Indiana, was the site of one of only two battles of the Civil War fought on Northern soil, the other being Gettysburg. When I learned this, I immediately decided to shift the setting for this last journal to Corydon.

Andrew Carter is fictional, as are the other young people who were involved in the debate scene. However, their debate represented some very real sentiment. By 1863 the Civil War was very unpopular throughout the Union. President Abraham Lincoln's popularity was very low. In fact, at the time, he was certain that he would not be re-elected in 1864. Debates like the one I wrote took place in cities and towns throughout the North.

General John Hunt Morgan's raid is real. My accounts of his raid into Indiana are based on fact. The Home Guard in the Corydon area was indeed commanded by Colonel Lewis Jordan. The accounts of the training drills of the new recruits are based on my understanding of the way Civil War soldiers were actually drilled.

The accounts of the actual battle and the subsequent capture of the Home Guard and ransacking of Corydon, including the killing of the county commissioner at the courthouse, are all based on factual events.

Glossary

Abolitionist: A person who was against slavery and who worked to bring it to an end.

Allegiance: Loyalty to a person, group, or cause.

Allowed: A slang term for assumed, as in "I allowed you'd be done by now."

Ascent: Rising up a slope or path.

Bandoleer: A shoulder belt with pockets for carrying ammunition.

Barter: Trading goods or services without using money.

Bayonet: A long knife that attaches to the end of a rifle, used in close combat.

Blockade: The blocking of a place to prevent anyone from entering or exiting.

Booty: Items stolen in a robbery.

Bough: Tree branch.

Cacophony: A loud mixture of harsh sounds.

Cain-tuck-ee: A term used by early pioneers and Native Americans to describe what is now Kentucky.

Chevron: A shape consisting of stripes meeting at an angle, similar to a wide, flattened v-shape.

Coffer: A storage place for money and valuables.

Consumption: A term for tuberculosis.

Contingency: An event that may or may not occur.

Countenance: A person's facial expression.

Crevasse: A deep opening or crack.

Cryptic: Secret or mysterious.

Descend: Going down a slope or path.

Desecrate: To treat a sacred place or object with disrespect.

Drawl: Speaking with drawn-out vowel sounds.

Edifice: A large, impressive structure.

Encroaching: Entering a place that is off-limits.

Felling: Cutting down, as with a tree.

Flense: The process of scraping fatty tissue from the underside of an animal hide in preparation for tanning.

Futile: Useless or hopeless.

Headwaters: The source of a stream or river.

Huzzah: An exclamation of excitement, similar to "Hooray!"

Imminent: About to happen.

Infamous: Famous for a negative reason.

Insurmountable: Unable to be overcome.

Knickers: Loose-fitting short pants, gathered at the knees.

Macabre: Gruesome or horrible.

Maritime: Related to the sea.

Marooned: Stranded.

Mason-Dixon Line: Originally the boundary line between Maryland and Pennsylvania, but now used figuratively to describe the dividing line between North and South.

Massa: Slang for "master," or plantation owner.

Meandering: Wandering back and forth.

Mercantile: A store that sells general trade goods.

Moons: Native American term for months.

Muster: In the military, the act of gathering men together to sign up for military service or for examination or inspection.

Notorious: Well known for negative reasons.

Obsessive-compulsive: Term used to describe a personality that needs to have everything in perfect order.

Palisade: A high fence constructed of pointed posts.

Plagiarize: To use the work of someone else and claim it as one's own.

Plunder: To loot or rob.

Polarizing: Something that is controversial and causes strong debate.

Prophetic: A statement that correctly predicts the future.

Protrude: Sticks out.

Provisions: Supplies.

Pungent: Having a strong odor.

Ransack: To tear up a place looking for something.

Ransom: A price paid to free someone being held captive.

Rebs: Short for Rebels, a slang term used to describe Confederate soldiers.

Regimen: A way of doing something the same way every time.

Rendezvous: A secret meeting.

Sanctioned: Officially approved.

Scalping: The act of removing the top portion of someone's hair and scalp to save as a battle trophy.

Scenario: A sequence of events.

Siege: To surround and shut off a location for a prolonged period of time in order to take control of it.

Soliloquy: A speech in which the speaker seems to be talking to himself or an unseen audience.

Spigot: Faucet.

Spile: A spigot used to tap maple trees that allows the sap to flow from the tree into a collection pail.

Stealthy: Quiet and sneaky.

Sweat equity: The value of a job resulting from the hard work put into it.

Tarred and feathered: A form of punishment in which a person is smeared with hot tar and covered with feathers.

Tedious: Long and boring.

Tenuous: Slight or insubstantial.

Treason: Action taken against one's own country.

Ulterior motive: A secret or hidden reason for doing something.

Viscous: Something sticky and semifluid.

Vista: A grand scenic view.

Selected Bibliography

Books

Aller, Susan Biven. *Tecumseh*. New York: Barnes and Noble Books, 2004.

Barrett, Carole, and Harvey Markowitz, eds. *American Indian Biographies*. Pasadena, CA: Salem Press, 2005.

Beller, Susan Provost. *The Revolutionary War*. New York: Benchmark Books, 2003.

Bial, Raymond. *The Shawnee*. New York: Benchmark Books, 2007.

Bobrick, Benson. *Fight for Freedom: The American Revolutionary War*. New York: Anthenaeum Books for Young Readers, 2004.

Brown, John Mason. *Daniel Boone: The Opening of the Wilderness*. New York: Sterling, 2007.

Burgan, Michael. *George Rogers Clark: American General*. Philadelphia: Chelsea House, 2002.

Cannavale, Matthew C. *North Carolina, 1524–1776*. Washington, DC: National Geographic, 2007.

Carey, Charles W., Jr. *The Mexican-American War: "Mr. Polk's War."* Berkeley Heights, NJ: Enslow, 2002.

Catel, Patrick. *The Home Front of the Revolutionary War*. Chicago: Heinemann Library, 2011.

Collier, Christopher, and James Lincoln Collier. *The French and Indian War, 1660–1763*. Tarrytown, NY: Benchmark Books, 1998.

Conley, Robert J. *Cherokee Thoughts: Honest and Uncensored*. Norman: University of Oklahoma Press, 2008.

Conway, W. Fred. *Corydon: The Forgotten Battle of the Civil War*. New Albany, IN: FBH, 1991.

Crenshaw, Gwendolyn J. *"Bury Me in a Free Land": The Abolitionist Movement in Indiana, 1816–1865*. Indianapolis: Indiana Historical Bureau, 1986.

Derzipilski, Kathleen. *Indiana*. New York: Benchmark Books, 2007.

Domnauer, Teresa. *Westward Expansion*. New York: Children's Press, 2010.

Donald, David Herbert. *Lincoln*. New York: Simon and Schuster, 1995.

Duke, Basil W. *A History of Morgan's Cavalry*. Bloomington: Indiana University Press, 1960.

Eckert, Allan W. *The Frontiersman*. Ashland, KY: Jesse Stuart Foundation, 2001.

———. *The Wilderness Empire*. Ashland, KY: Jesse Stuart Foundation, 2001.

———. *The Wilderness War*. Ashland, KY: Jesse Stuart Foundation, 2003.

Etter, John P. *The Indiana Legion: A Civil War Militia*. Carmel, IN: Hawthorne Publishing, 2006.

Fatout, Paul. *Indiana Canals*. West Lafayette, IN: Purdue University Press, 1972.

Feldman, Ruth Tenzer. *The Mexican-American War*. Minneapolis: Lerner Publications, 2004.

Fradin, Dennis B. *The Underground Railroad*. New York: Marshall Cavendish Benchmark, 2008.

Garman, Harry Otto. *Whitewater Canal: Cambridge City to the Ohio River*. n. p. [1944].

Gerson, Noel Bertram. *Franklin: America's "Lost State."* New York: Crowell–Collier Press, 1968.

Giles, Janice Holt. *The Kentuckians*. Lexington: University of Kentucky Press, 1988.

Gleitz, Karen. *Historic Corydon, from A to Z: A Guidebook to Corydon's Historical Sites*. Evansville, IN: M. T. Publishing, 2005.

Hamilton, Sue. *Blackbeard*. Edina, MN: ABDO, 2007.

Katz, William Loren. *Black Pioneers: An Untold Story*. New York: Anthenaeum Books for Young Readers, 1999.

Laager, Hollie. *The French and Indian War*. Vero Beach, FL: Rourke Publishing, 2007.

Lasky, Kathryn. *Sugaring Time*. New York: Aladdin Books, 1986.

Lund, Bill. *The Cherokee Indians*. Mankato, MN: Bridgestone Books, 1997.

Macdonald, Fiona. *Top Ten Worst Nasty Pirates You Wouldn't Want to Meet*. New York: Gareth Stevens, 2007.

Maynard, Charles W. *The Appalachians*. New York: Powerkids Press, 2004.

McAmis, Herb. *The Cherokee*. Austin, TX: Raintree Steck-Vaughn, 2000.

Morgan, Robert. *Boone: A Biography*. Chapel Hill, NC: Algonquin Books, 2008.

Operations of the Indiana Legion and Minute Men, 1863–4: Documents to the General Assembly, with the Governor's Message, January 6, 1865. Indianapolis: W. R. Holloway, 1865.

Osborn, William M. *The Wild Frontier: Atrocities During the American-Indian War from Jamestown Colony to Wounded Knee*. New York: Random House, 2000.

Otfinoski, Steven. *William Henry Harrison: America's Ninth President*. Encyclopedia of Presidents. New York: Children's Press, 2003.

Report of Major General Love, of the Indiana Legion. Indianapolis: J. J. Bingham, 1863.

Roberts, Russell. *Daniel Boone*. Hockesinn, DE: Mitchell Lane, 2007.

Shirley, David, and Joyce Hart. *North Carolina*. 2nd ed. New York: Marshall Cavendish Benchmark, 2010.

Somes, Joseph Henry Vanderburgh. *Old Vincennes: The History of a Famous Old Town and Its Glorious Past*. New York: Graphic Books, 1962.

Stanchak, John. *Civil War*. Rev. ed. New York: Dorling Kindersley, 2011.

Swain, Gwenyth. *President of the Underground Railroad: A Story about Levi Coffin*. Minneapolis: Carolrhoda Books, 2001.

Taylor, David L. *"With Bowie Knives and Pistols": Morgan's Raid in Indiana*. Lexington, IN: TaylorMade Write, 1993.

Thom, James Alexander. *Follow the River*. New York: Ballantine Books, 1981.

———. *Long Knife*. New York: Ballantine Books, 1994.

———. *Panther in the Sky*. New York: Ballantine Books, 1990.

Waxman, Laura Hamilton. *How Did Slaves Find a Route to Freedom? And Other Questions about the Underground Railroad*. Minneapolis: Lerner, 2011.

Weber, Jennifer L. *Copperheads: The Rise and Fall of Lincoln's Opponents in the North.* Oxford: Oxford University Press, 2006.

Williams, Samuel Cole. *History of the Lost State of Franklin.* Philadelphia: Porcupine Press, 1974.

Williams, Ted. *Big Medicine from Six Nations.* Syracuse, NY: Syracuse University Press, 2007.

Worth, Richard. *North Carolina.* Life in the Thirteen Colonies. New York: Children's Press, 2004.

Internet Sources

National Park Service. "CWSAC Battle Summaries: Corydon." http://www.nps.gov /history/hps/abpp/battles/in001.htm.

"Battle of Corydon, Indiana." *CivilWarAlbum.* http://www.civilwaralbum.com/misc3 /corydon1.htm.

Beard, Reed. *The Battle of Tippecanoe.* Chicago: W. B. Conkey, 1911. Transcription, USGenWeb. http://usgwarchives.net/ky/tippecanoe/.

Civil War Indiana. http://civilwarindiana.com/.

Daniel Boone Wilderness Trail Association. http://danielboonetrail.com/.

Historic Metamora, Indiana. http://www.metamoraindiana.com/.

Indiana State Museum. "The Whitewater Canal." http://www.indianamuseum.org /explore/whitewater-canal.

The Blowing Rock. "The Legend of the Blowing Rock." http://theblowingrock.com /legend.html.

North Carolina Maritime Museums. http://www.ncmaritimemuseums.com/.

North Carolina Museum of History. "North Carolina American Indian History Time Line." http://www.ncdcr.gov/ncmoh/learn/ForEducators/Timelines/North CarolinaAmericanIndianHistoryTimeLine.aspx.

Tennessee Historical Society and the University of Tennessee. *The Tennessee Encyclopedia of History and Culture.* http://tennesseeencyclopedia.net/.

Tennessee History for Kids. http://www.tnhistoryforkids.org/.

Tipton–Haynes State Historic Site. http://tipton-haynes.org/.

North Carolina Office of Archives and History and the University of North Carolina Press. "Natives and Newcomers: North Carolina Before 1770: The Tuscarora Wars." http:// www.waywelivednc.com/before-1770/tuscarora-war.htm.

Whitewater Canal Trail. "History." http://www.whitewatercanaltrail.com/History.php.

Multimedia

Weber, Robert. *Bicycling through History: Revolutionary Period, Across the Appalachians.* DVD, 2004.

Subject Index by Chapter